Little Passports®
50 STATES
WORKBOOK

ALABAMA
The Yellowhammer State

Capital: **Montgomery** * Abbreviation: **AL**
22nd State: **Joined December 14, 1819**

Alabama was named after the **ALABAMA TRIBE**, a group of indigenous people who lived on the land at the time of European settlement. The Alabamas made pottery, rivercane baskets, and wood carvings. Native American pottery features different variations and combinations of the designs shown in the key. For example, some pots have stripes, some have circles, and some have both stripes and circles.

WHICH POTS DON'T BELONG?

Circle the pots that do not use any of the designs in the key; these do not belong in this collection of Native American pottery. Count the circled pots to learn a fact about Alabama.

DESIGN KEY

Stripes
Crosshatching
Waves
Indents
Circles

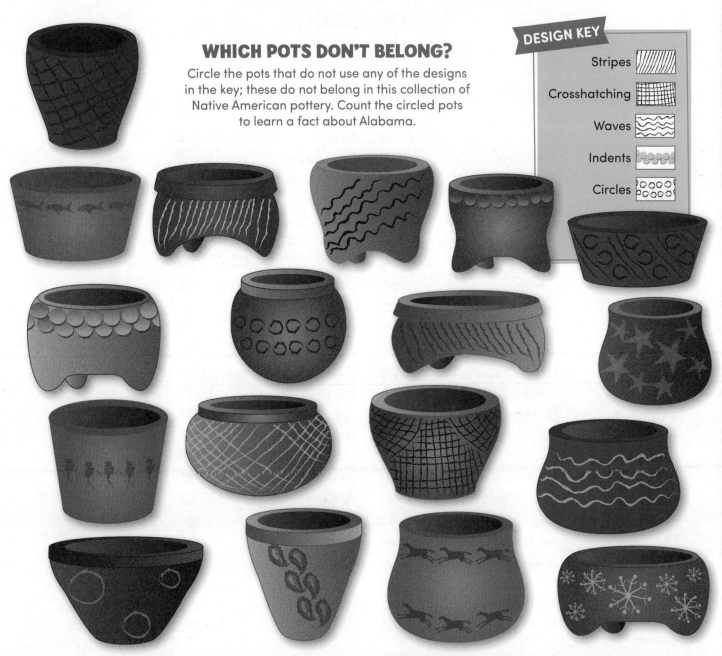

The name "Alabama" is believed to come from the Choctaw words *alba amo*, meaning:
4 sea fisher   6 thicket clearer   8 mountain traveler   10 shelter builder

U.S. SPACE & ROCKET CENTER
HUNTSVILLE, AL

Visitors can sign up for Space Camp to learn about space, aviation, robotics, cyber technologies, and more. Hundreds of thousands of students have been to Space Camp since the center opened in 1982.

Visitors can view a replica of a space shuttle and learn about space launches throughout history!

At what time should launch preparations begin?

Go through the checklist to find out!

9:35 p.m
YOUR ANSWER

LAUNCH CHECKLIST

✓ Sam and Sofia's space launch is at 4:55 p.m.

✓ It takes 3 hours to fill the shuttle's fuel tank.

✓ After the tank is filled, Sam and Sofia take 30 minutes to suit up.

✓ It takes 10 minutes for them to board the ship.

✓ It takes 30 minutes for them to prepare the shuttle flight deck.

IDENTIFY THE SPACE CAMPERS

Five campers have suited up for simulation in the space shuttle. They line up so an engineer can inspect their suits, but two of them aren't finished suiting up. Use the clues to figure out each camper's place in line and to determine who needs more time to get ready. Complete the diagram as you read the clues.

CLUES

The two campers who need more time to get ready are standing second and fifth in line.

Kerry doesn't need any more time, but she's standing to the left of a camper who does.

Sarah and Elliot need more time.

Sarah stands between two campers who don't need more time.

Brock stands to the left of Jude.

① Jude
CAMPER NAME
Needs more time
Yes ☐ No ☑

② sarah
CAMPER NAME
Needs more time
Yes ☑ No ☐

③ Brock
CAMPER NAME
Needs more time
Yes ☐ No ☑

④ kerry
CAMPER NAME
Needs more time
Yes ☐ No ☑

⑤ Elliot
CAMPER NAME
Needs more time
Yes ☑ No ☑

ALASKA
✳ The Last Frontier ✳

Capital: **Juneau** • Abbreviation: **AK**
49th State: **Joined January 3, 1959**

ALASKAN ANIMAL TRACKS

Animals in Alaska walk, crawl, gallop, and hop through a variety of conditions and habitats. Their paws, hooves, and webbed feet must be able to travel over icy snow, rocky slopes, forested woodlands, and sea-swept coasts.

HUNT FOR TRACKS

Draw a line to lead each animal to its matching animal tracks.

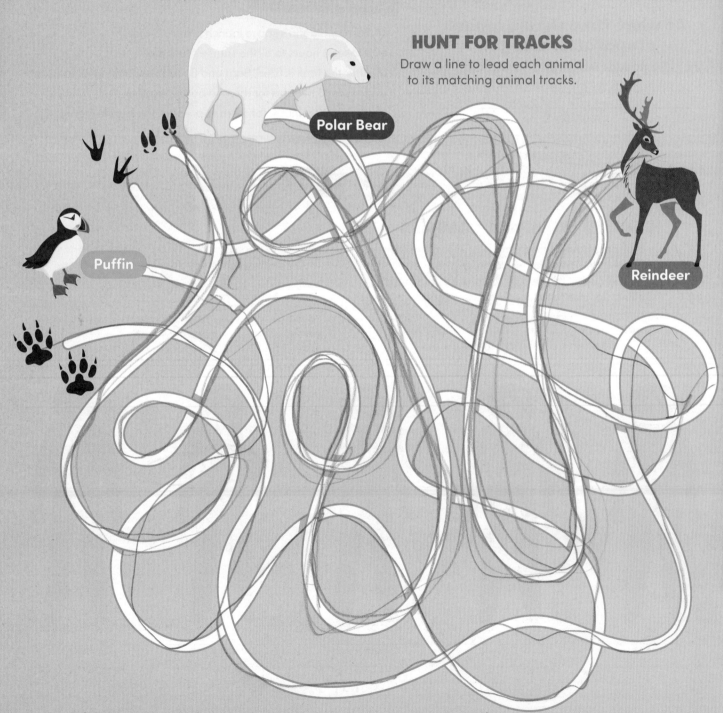

Polar Bear

Puffin

Reindeer

ALASKAN LIGHT SHOW

THE AURORA BOREALIS (also called the northern lights) is a mesmerizing natural phenomenon that creates rippling bursts of vibrant color in Alaska's night sky.

Count all the stars on this page and look at the glacier below to learn what creates this amazing Alaskan light show!

Other places you can see the aurora borealis:

Canada   Sweden

Iceland   Finland

Greenland   Norway

What causes the aurora borealis?

15 stars = ice crystals sparkling within clouds

25 stars = moonlight reflecting off the ice of glaciers and icebergs

35 stars = particles from the sun reacting with gases in the atmosphere

45 stars = solar activity far off in space

ARIZONA
✳ The Grand Canyon State ✳

Capital: **Phoenix**   Abbreviation: **AZ**
48ᵗʰ State: **Joined February 14, 1912**

PETRIFIED FOREST NATIONAL PARK
is known for the 220 million-year-old fossilized trees found throughout its rocky landscape.

The trees in this region most likely grew year-round, but some species can store information about their lives in their trunks! The number of rings on the stumps below tell you the age of each tree, with each ring representing one year of the tree's life.

17

5

9

20

Count the rings and write the age of each tree in the blank boxes.

Add the total number of rings to learn the name of the desert where the petrified forest is located. Circle the correct answer below.

59 The Sonoran Desert

61 The Painted Desert

64 The Mojave Desert

Let's Draw!

Gila Monster

Grab a blank piece of paper and draw some gila monsters: poisonous but gentle lizards that live in Arizona's deserts.

① ② ③ ④

ARIZONA WILDLIFE

Directions

1. Place a lamp next to a blank wall and turn it on.
2. Sit or stand between the lamp and the wall.
3. Try to bend your fingers to mirror the shapes in each picture. The closer your hands are to the light, the larger your shadows will be. The farther away your hands are, the smaller your shadows will be.

Use your hands to make shadow puppets of five animals from Arizona!

Roadrunners belong to the cuckoo bird family. With long, powerful legs, they prefer running to flying.

Javelinas (pronounced hah-vuh-*LEE*-nuh) look like wild boars with white hairlines around their necks. They feed on prickly pear cacti, including the spines!

Coyotes are smaller than wolves and are often mistaken for dogs. Coyotes live all over Arizona.

Desert cottontail rabbits are named for their small tails that look like white cotton balls. These rabbits can be found in Arizona's deserts.

Hawks are a common sight in Arizona. They are known for their incredible speed and their ability to dive in midair to catch small prey.

ARKANSAS

✳ The Natural State ✳

Capital: **Little Rock** ✳ Abbreviation: **AR**
25th State: **Joined June 15, 1836**

CRATER OF DIAMONDS STATE PARK is the only public park in the world
where you can go hunting for diamonds. If you find one of these precious stones, you get to keep it!

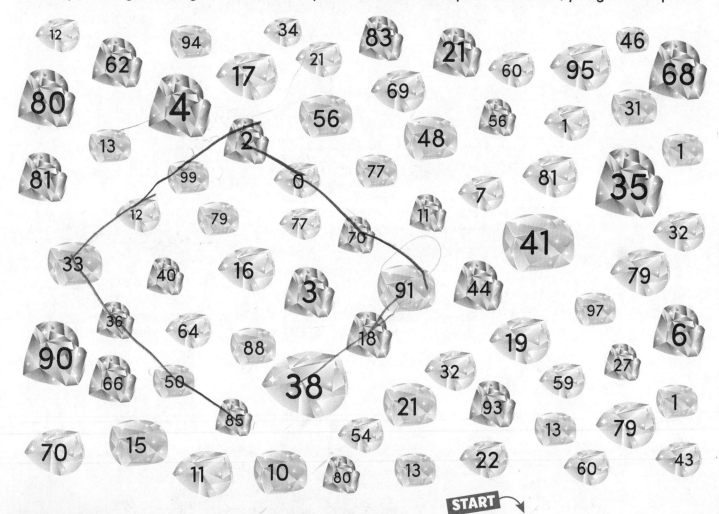

Step 1: Find and circle the equations' answers in the diamond field.

Step 2: Starting with 85, draw a line from one answer to the next closest answer.

Step 3: Find the white diamond in the center of the shape created by the connected answers. This number will complete the weight of the largest diamond found in the park!

$(12 \times 10) - 35 = \underline{85}$　　$11 + 73 - 82 = \underline{2}$

$(9 \div 9) \times 50 = \underline{50}$　　$(45 \div 3) - 15 = \underline{0}$

$(8 - 5) \times 12 = \underline{36}$　　$(86 + 7) - 23 = \underline{70}$

$(5 + 28) \times 1 = \underline{33}$　　$(9 \times 3) + 64 = \underline{91}$

$(0 \times 83) + 12 = \underline{12}$　　$(33 \div 11) + 15 = \underline{18}$

$(56 - 23) \times 3 = \underline{99}$　　$92 - 15 - 39 = \underline{38}$

Did You Know?
Diamonds are measured in carats. Each carat equals 200 milligrams, which is about the same weight as 10 grains of rice.

The largest diamond found in Crater of Diamonds State Park weighed ___38___**.37 carats.**

8

BIKING IN THE OUACHITA MOUNTAINS

There are many natural landmarks in Arkansas named after the Ouachita (pronounced WAH-shi-taw) Native American tribe. The Ouachita National Forest, the Ouachita Mountains, the Ouachita River, and Lake Ouachita are all popular travel destinations for nature lovers.

Jeff

Lucy

Tim

Mia

Mitch

Trace each biker's trail to see who completed the entire route.

Mountain bikers face challenging and steep trails at the Ouachita Mountains. Only the most experienced bikers bike all the way to the top of the trails.

CALIFORNIA
✳ The Golden State ✳

Capital: **Sacramento** ✳ Abbreviation: **CA**
31st State: **Joined September 9, 1850**

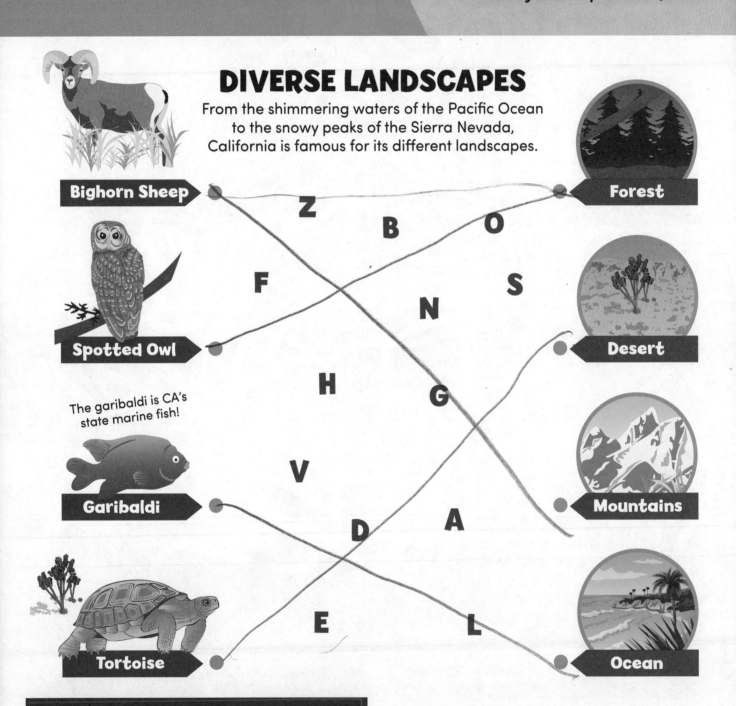

DIVERSE LANDSCAPES

From the shimmering waters of the Pacific Ocean to the snowy peaks of the Sierra Nevada, California is famous for its different landscapes.

Bighorn Sheep

Spotted Owl

The garibaldi is CA's state marine fish!

Garibaldi

Tortoise

Z B O

F S

N

H G

V

D A

E L

Forest

Desert

Mountains

Ocean

WHAT IS THE STATE MINERAL?

Drawing in straight lines, connect the animals on the left with their matching habitats on the right. Each line will cross a letter. Write the letters in the blanks to learn California's state mineral.

California's state mineral is

G O L D

A mineral is a solid, naturally occurring substance found in the earth.

Draw and color your very own horse on a blank sheet of paper. Start by sketching the lines and shapes. Color them in as you go.

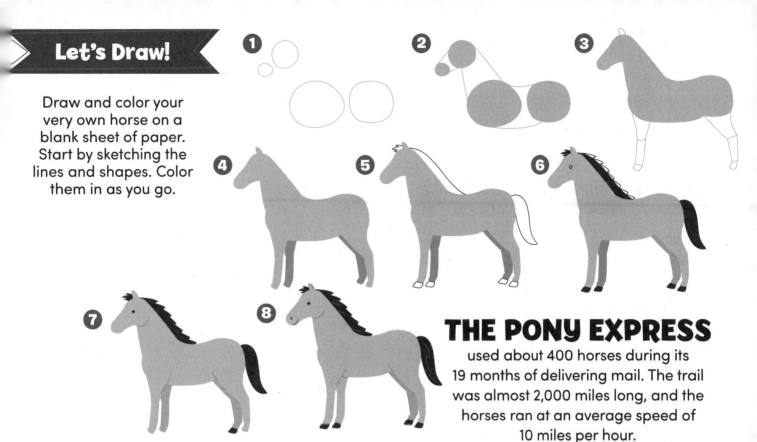

THE PONY EXPRESS

used about 400 horses during its 19 months of delivering mail. The trail was almost 2,000 miles long, and the horses ran at an average speed of 10 miles per hour.

THE CALIFORNIA GOLD RUSH

began when James W. Marshall found gold at Sutter's Mill in Coloma. Thousands of miners came to California to search for gold. Miners sifted through river rocks with special pans and excavated gold particles from bluffs and hillsides.

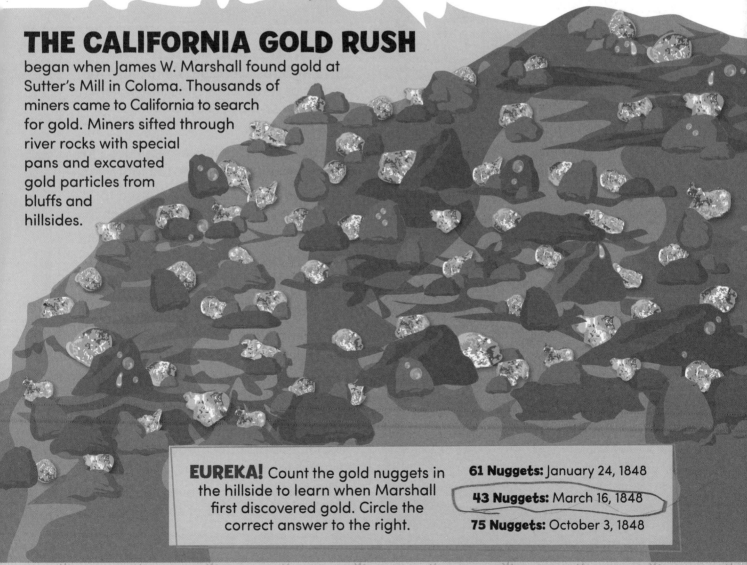

EUREKA! Count the gold nuggets in the hillside to learn when Marshall first discovered gold. Circle the correct answer to the right.

61 Nuggets: January 24, 1848

43 Nuggets: March 16, 1848

75 Nuggets: October 3, 1848

COLORADO
✳ The Centennial State ✳

Capital: **Denver** ✳ Abbreviation: **CO**
38th State: **Joined August 1, 1876**

MESA VERDE NATIONAL PARK

is known for the ancient homes built into some of the area's large rocks and cliffsides. The largest of these homes has 150 rooms and is called the Cliff Palace.

Researchers have found many artifacts here over the years, some of which are made of yucca plants. These discoveries help scientists understand more about the Ancestral Pueblo people who built these homes between the 12th and 13th centuries.

There are many species of yucca, some of which have medicinal properties, like lowering inflammation and treating sore joints.

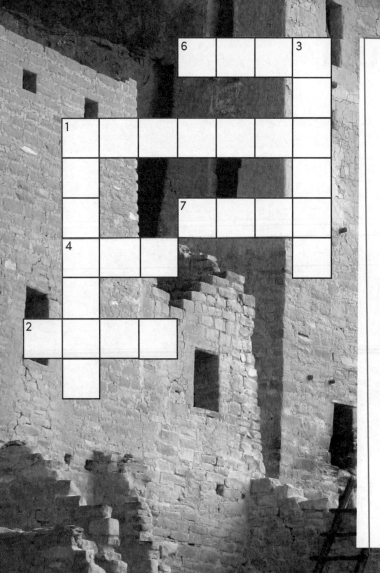

USEFUL YUCCA

Solve the crossword puzzle to learn the names of some of the household items found by researchers.

Across

1. Yucca fibers from leaves were used to weave this type of open-toe footwear.

2. Chopped yucca roots were used to create this cleaning product, which is good for washing hands.

4. When dried, fibers from yucca leaves can be made into this flat item that is generally placed on the floor.

6. Yucca leaves are strong enough to make this type of baby furniture.

7. Dry yucca plants made excellent kindling for starting a _____.

Down

1. Chopped, squashed, and mixed with water, this product made of yucca root is used for washing hair.

3. The fibers in yucca leaves can be woven into this type of container.

COOL-ORADO ANIMALS

Animals that are more active at night than during the day are called nocturnal. Animals that are active in daylight are called diurnal. Can you tell which animals on this page are nocturnal and which are diurnal?

Pair the animals with their correct habitats. Read the description of each animal and draw a line to its matching national park.

Rocky Mountain National Park has at least 60 mountain peaks higher than 12,000 feet.

Hummingbirds spend several months in this habitat to stock up for a long migration. They feed on flower nectars and small insects during the day.

Bighorn sheep travel easily through rugged lands thanks to their split hooves. You can spot them fighting other bighorn sheep during the day.

Great Sand Dunes National Park is known for its enormous sloping sand dunes, which are the tallest in North America.

Tiger salamanders stay out of sight during the day and venture from their hiding places at night. Because they breed in water, tiger salamanders prefer to live in swampy canyons.

Mesa Verde National Park attracts migrating wildlife to the protective cubbies of its ancient cliff dwellings.

Kangaroo rats can live their entire lives without drinking water. Named after kangaroos because of their high jumping abilities, these rats are active in the dark.

Black Canyon of the Gunnison National Park is famous for its steep canyon walls that drop down to the Gunnison River.

CONNECTICUT
The Nutmeg State

Capital: Hartford ✳ **Abbreviation: CT**
5th State: **Joined January 9, 1788**

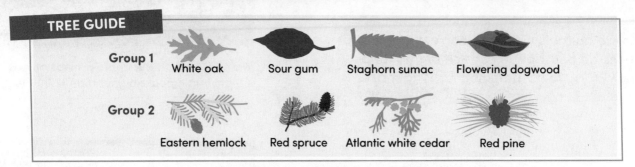

TREE GUIDE

Group 1: White oak, Sour gum, Staghorn sumac, Flowering dogwood

Group 2: Eastern hemlock, Red spruce, Atlantic white cedar, Red pine

IDENTIFY THE TREES

Using the tree guide, find and circle each tree sequence. Make sure you only circle the tree sequences where each leaf or pine branch is featured in exactly the same order as shown in the guide. The groups might appear horizontally, vertically, or diagonally. When you finish, fill in the group number at the bottom of the page based on the number of times it appears in the puzzle to reveal each group's scientific name.

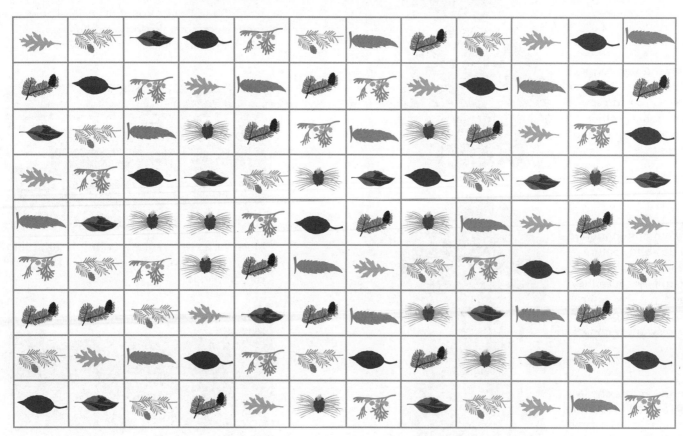

Group _____ appears three times in the puzzle.
Trees in this group usually shed leaves seasonally and are called **deciduous** trees.

Group _____ appears two times in the puzzle.
Trees in this group keep their foliage throughout most of their life cycle and are called **evergreen** trees.

14

EXPLORING THE FOREST

ABOUT 60% OF CONNECTICUT IS COVERED BY FORESTS. Once cleared and used for farming, much of the emerald-green forests of the Constitution State have regrown since the 1800s.

Follow the **odd** numbers out of the center of the forest! Shade in the bubble at the end of the path to mark the correct exit. Hint: Keep a sharp eye out! Some odd numbers might lead you down the wrong path.

DELAWARE
✳ The First State ✳

Capital: **Dover** ✳ Abbreviation: **DE**
1st State: **Joined December 7, 1787**

LADYBUGS!

In 1974, students at an elementary school in Milford convinced lawmakers to designate the ladybug as the Delaware state insect.

Solve the number puzzle below to learn some fun facts about ladybugs.

1	6	5	7	9	4		3	8
4		7			2		5	
9					6			4
8	1		4		5			2
5	7	6	2		9			
2			6		1			5
3		1	5		7	8	4	9
6	9					5	2	7
	5			2	8	1		3

INSTRUCTIONS

Fill in the empty squares with numbers 1 through 9. Each row, column, and square must contain these numbers, but they cannot be repeated in any row, column, or square more than once.

Tip 1: Start with the rows and columns that have the most numbers already in them.

Tip 2: Use a pencil with an eraser.

Fun Facts

When you finish the puzzle, look at the numbers in the shaded squares. Circle those same numbers in the list of fun facts below. The one number that isn't circled lists a false fact about ladybugs. Cross it out!

1. Ladybugs protect crops by eating tiny plant pests.
2. Ladybugs are called **lady beetles** and **ladybirds** by some people.
3. There are about 5,000 different ladybug species.
4. The red color of ladybugs attracts predators.
5. When in danger, ladybugs can play dead.

PLAYIN' CHICKEN

One of these species of chickens is the Delaware state bird. It's such a big part of Delaware state culture, in fact, it's a university mascot!

A Buckeye

B White Leghorn

1 Complete each pattern by writing the correct chicken's letter in each blank box. The chicken that correctly completes the most patterns is the state bird!

2 Write the correct chicken's name in the blank to learn the name of the University of Delaware's mascot.

C Blue Hen

D Cochin

The University of Delaware's _____

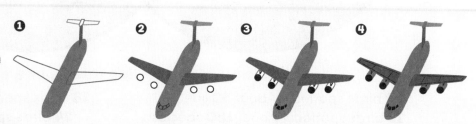

Let's Draw!

The Air Mobility Command Museum on Dover Air Force Base has a collection of retired planes. Draw one of them, following these steps.

❶ **❷** **❸** **❹**

FLORIDA

✳ The Sunshine State ✳

Capital: **Tallahassee** ✳ Abbreviation: **FL**
27th State: **Joined March 3, 1845**

EVERGLADES NATIONAL PARK is home to countless plants, insects, and animals, including a variety of species of mammals, reptiles, fish, and, of course, birds! It's a favorite spot for birdwatchers who spend hours exploring the swamps hoping to find their favorite species.

GO BIRD WATCHING!

Look through the binoculars and count all the birds in both views. The correct number will tell you a fun fact about this amazing natural park.

The **bald eagle** is one of the most common birds of prey seen in the Everglades.

Wading birds are often seen perched in tall trees when not hunting for food.

The **ruby-throated hummingbird** eats nectar, spiders, and small insects.

Woodpeckers build their nests in holes they peck into trees.

The **jewel of the marsh** is named after its vibrantly colored feathers.

Wading birds like the **spoonbill** fish for food in shallow, warm waters.

How many bird species live in the Everglades?

12 birds spotted = About **50** species!

15 birds spotted = About **180** species!

18 birds spotted = More than **300** species!

24 birds spotted = About **420** species!

CLUES

Where NASA sends rockets and astronauts

Something that isn't being used; extra

To look at something or someone intensely

Not new or fresh; an old piece of bread

A strong post or spike used to anchor a tent

A slithery reptile that doesn't have limbs

Something to nibble on between meals

When a rope is loose; the opposite of taut

Smooth or slippery, and usually wet

A single piece of bread

Something to add flavor to food

Where NASA sends rockets and astronauts

THE KENNEDY SPACE CENTER

is located in Cape Canaveral and has been the home of America's space exploration for decades. NASA launches rockets from platforms near the space center and also used to launch space shuttles from this same location.

Use the clues to fill in the blanks and complete the word ladder.

Each word is only allowed to have **one different letter** from the previous word.

Hint: The first and final words have already been added for you. The correct sequence will end in SPACE, where you began.

GEORGIA
The Peach State

Capital: **Atlanta** ✳ Abbreviation: **GA**
4th State: **Joined January 2, 1788**

Learn some **GEORGIA FUN FACTS** by filling in the blanks below!
Write each letter from the top rows in the matching colored boxes beneath.

T	A	A	L	A	T	N

The capital of Georgia is . . .

H	S	N	V	A	A	N	A

This city is known for its old oak trees that are often draped with Spanish moss.

S	I	S	I	S	P	M	I	S	I	P

R	E	V	I	R

Georgia is the one of the largest states east of the . . .

T	R	I	N	M	A

U	E	H	T	R	L

I	N	G	K

R	J

This civil rights leader was born in Georgia, and his legacy lives on today through the actions of everyone who continues to fight for racial equality.

GEORGIA IS ONE OF THE NATION'S TOP PRODUCERS OF PEACHES AND PEANUTS.

It's so famous for its peaches, in fact, "Georgia peach" is a common phrase used around the country to describe the fruit itself and the kind people who live in the Peach State.

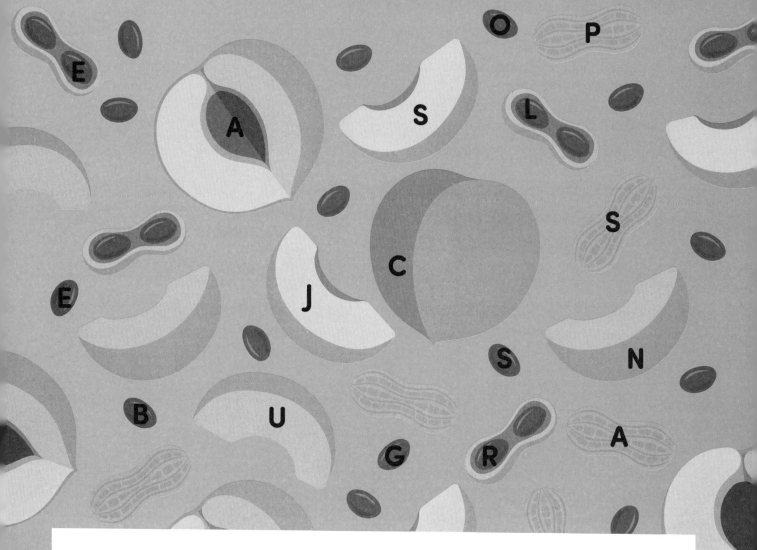

FIND THE LETTERS hidden among the produce and write them in the blanks below using the images as clues!

Peanuts aren't the only nuts grown in the Peach State!

More  are harvested in Georgia than in

any other state, mostly in the months of October and November.

Capital: Honolulu   Abbreviation: HI
50th State: **Joined August 21, 1959**

ENGLISH AND HAWAIIAN are Hawaii's two official languages.

Find the 10 words and their English translations in the word search. Each Hawaiian word will share a letter with its English translation. See our example for **mahalo**, which means "thank you." Complete the word list with the English translations after you find all the words.
Hint: Words appear horizontally, vertically, and diagonally.

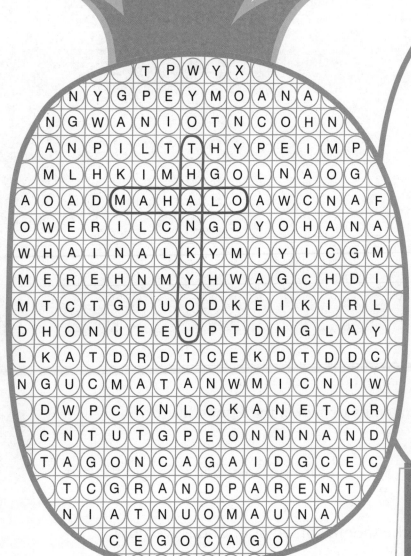

	Hawaiian	English
1.	MAHALO	THANK YOU
2.	MOANA	_____
3.	KEIKI	_____
4.	OHANA	_____
5.	KUPUNA	_____
6.	AINA	_____
7.	MAUNA	_____
8.	HONU	_____
9.	KANE	_____
10.	WAHINE	_____

Fun Fact!
The pineapple resembles a native Hawaiian fruit called *hala*. The Hawaiian name for pineapple is *hala kahiki*, which means "foreign hala."

HUMPBACK WHALES make the long journey from Alaska to Hawaii every year to give birth in the warm waters of Hawaii. Did you know baby whales are called **calves**?

> When a whale leaps out of the water, it is called **breaching**.

ORIGAMI WHALE
Follow these instructions to make your own whale.

Materials
☐ 6x6-inch square colored paper ☐ Scissors ☐ Crayons

Instructions

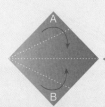

1. Fold the square in half, crease, and unfold.
2. Fold corners A and B inside so they meet at the center fold line.
3. Fold corner C inside so it meets corners A and B.
4. Fold the paper in half.

5. Fold up corner D. It's your whale's tail.
6. Using scissors, make a short cut through the end of the tail and unfold its edges.
7. Using crayons, draw its eyes and fins. Your whale is complete!

WILD CHICKENS AND ROOSTERS roam the island of Kauai.
Find and circle the 10 differences on the roosters above.

IDAHO
The Gem State

Capital: **Boise**　Abbreviation: **ID**
43rd State: **Joined July 3, 1890**

FLY FISHING is a popular sport along the Boise River. To get closer to the fish, fishers usually wade into the water. Instead of bait, they use artificial flies to attract fish. These are special lures made with feathers and thread. They are so light, you have to whip your fishing line back and forth in order to cast it into the water.

UNTANGLE THE FISHING LINE!
Trace the line from the end of the pole to its artificial fly. The correct fly will tell you the name of the larger river the Boise River flows from.

Snake River　**Mississippi River**　**Payette River**

CRACK THE CODES!
Some popular places in and around Boise are listed below, but their names are in code! Decode the words using the given letters. Complete the alphabet as you go to help crack the code.

Decode the letters in the spaces below.

A	B	C	D	E	F	G	H	I	J	K	L	M	N	O	P	Q	R	S	T	U	V	W	X	Y	Z
M		S	Y			Q	F	Z			C	R	B	I	V		K	X				T	J	N	

↙ Decoded Letters

1
R _ C K Y
M U L R E

M _ N T _ I N S
B U G Y W K O Y D

2
B _ _ S _ B _ S I N
N U T G D N K D O Y

3
B _ I S _ R I _ _ R
N U O D C M O P C M

4
_ R _ _ C N T _ R F _ R
Z U M V Q L C Y W C M I U M

_ B I R _ S _ _ F _ _ R Y
N O M Q D U I F M C E

5
_ N N _ _ F R _ N K _ _ M _ N
K Y Y C I M K Y R A G B K Y

R I _ T S _ M M R I _
M O T A W D B C B U M O K V

6
I _ _ _ _ B _ T _ N I C _
O Q K A U N U W K Y O L K V

_ _ R _ _
T K M Q C Y

7
B _ I S _ _ N T I _ N
N U O D C Y K W O U Y K V

F _ R _ ST
I U M C D W

8
J _ _ I _
X G V O K

_ V I S _ _ _ R K
Q K P O D F K M R

9
_ _ C K Y _ _ _ K
V G L R E F C K R

_ _ M
Q K B

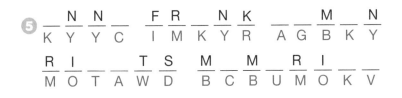

ILLINOIS
✳ The Prairie State ✳

Capital: Springfield ✳ **Abbreviation: IL**
21st State: Joined December 3, 1818

A SLICE OF ILLINOIS

Chicago deep-dish pizza is famous around the country for its flavor-loaded size and ingredients.

Complete the equations using the numbers that match the toppings.

What's wrong with this picture?

Even answer = True Chicago slices don't include any toppings! Just sauce, cheese, and doughy goodness!

Odd answer = Toppings on true Chicago slices are buried beneath the sauce, like tasty little surprises.

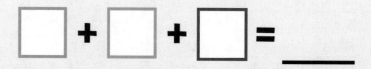

THE WINDY CITY

The origin of Chicago's nickname is a bit of a mystery! The most obvious explanation is Chicago's windy weather, but some believe the nickname was inspired by Chicago's talkative politicians, who were known to give long-winded speeches.

Solve the number puzzle below to learn which fun facts about Chicago are true and which are not.

1	3	6	2	4	7		8	9
2	5	8		1			7	6
4	7	9		6			2	1
6		4			3	2		8
8			4		2			
3		7	6			9		
5	4			2		7	9	3
7	6			3		8	4	5
	8	3	7	5		1		2

INSTRUCTIONS

Fill in the empty squares with numbers 1 through 9. Each row, column, and square must contain these numbers, but they cannot be repeated in any row, column, or square more than once.

Tip 1: Start with the rows and columns that have the most numbers already in them.

Tip 2: Use a pencil with an eraser.

When you finish, circle the numbers in the shaded squares and find them in the list below. The circled numbers represent true facts about the Windy City.

1. The first Ferris wheel was invented in Chicago.
2. Chicago's downtown area is called the Ring.
3. There are more than 550 parks in Chicago.
4. One of Chicago's many nicknames is the Bean Town.
5. The first car race in the USA was held in Illinois and ran from Chicago to Evanston and back.

INDIANA

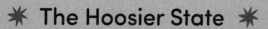

✳ The Hoosier State ✳

Capital: **Indianapolis** ✳ Abbreviation: **IN**
19th State: **Joined December 11, 1816**

Sloping mounds of sand, called **DUNES**, decorate the landscape throughout Indiana Dunes National Park.

COMPLETE THE FUN FACTS below to learn more about the dunes and the Hoosier State. Draw a line to connect each fact to its matching group of scrambled letter tiles. Hint: Use the images as clues!

The dunes are made of "_____" sand, which makes a unique sound when walked on.

A CI GL RS E

The dunes were created by receding _____.

S G IN G IN

The dunes are located near Lake _____.

O CR SS A O R DS

Indiana's state motto is "the "_____ of America."

HI C AN G MI

Indianapolis hosts a famous auto race called the _____ 500.

Y D IN

NATIVE AMERICAN PEOPLE are an important part

of Indiana culture. Many indigenous communities were pushed westward by European settlers in the 19th century, and, to preserve their contributions to the state, important native sites are protected today.

LOCATE FOUR NATIVE SITES

on the map by writing the correct number in each of the white stars.
Hint: Use the images as clues!

NATIVE SITES

 1 Mounds State Park

 2 Potts Creek Rockshelter

 3 Eiteljorg Museum

 4 Prophetstown State Park

LEGEND

 State Capital

 City

 Interstate

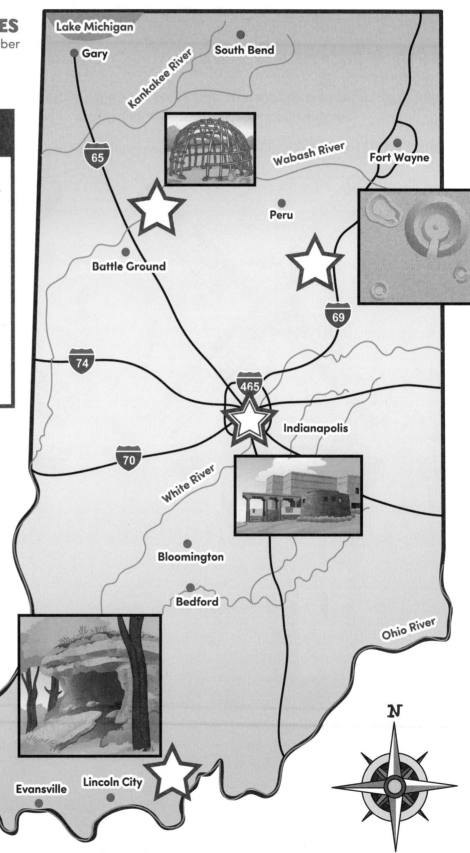

IOWA
✳ The Hawkeye State ✳

Capital: **Des Moines** ✳ Abbreviation: **IA**
29th State: **Joined December 28, 1846**

THE VERMEER MILL is one of the tallest working windmills in the USA. It was modeled after 19th-century windmills and is used to make flour, which is used for cooking in local bakeries and restaurants. You'll find windmills in the town of Pella, which is an old town (established in 1847 by Dutch immigrants) with many historical houses.

FIND THE 10 DIFFERENCES between the windmills below and learn a fun fact about the Dutch.

Fun Facts

How many differences did you discover on the **mill blades**? Match the number to the correct fun fact below.

1 Vermeer Mill is the oldest Dutch mill in the USA.

2 Red is the Dutch national color.

3 The Netherlands grows more tulips than any other country in the world. The tulip is one of the symbols of Dutch culture.

THE LOESS HILLS

In the western part of Iowa, there are some rare land formations known as the Loess Hills. The hills were formed thousands of years ago from windblown dust and silt. These types of hills are known as loess deposits and can also be found in Europe and Asia.

Loess deposits are soft and crumbly. They are considered very good for agriculture because they are full of minerals. The thickest loess hills in the world are near the Missouri River in Iowa and the Yellow River in China. Hiking and wildlife viewing are popular activities in the Loess Hills of Iowa.

Let's Draw!

Draw and color your very own wild turkey on a blank sheet of paper. Follow the steps below. Start by sketching the lines and shapes. Color them in as you go.

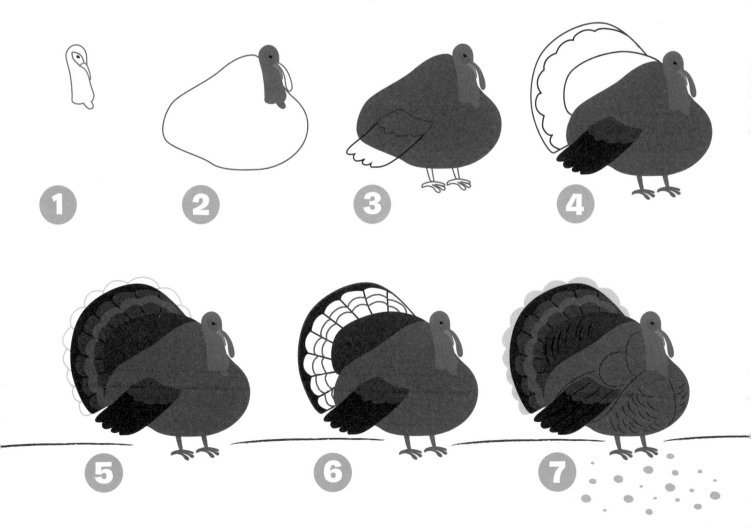

1
2
3
4
5
6
7

31

KANSAS
❋ The Sunflower State ❋

Capital: **Topeka** ❋ Abbreviation: **KS**
34th State: **Joined January 29, 1861**

KANSAS INVENTIONS

In 1872, Dr. Brewster M. Higley, inspired by his peaceful life in Smith County, Kansas, wrote a poem called "The Western Home." The words later became the lyrics for the state song of Kansas, "Home on the Range." The song, beginning with the lyric "Oh, give me a home where the buffalo roam," is one of the most famous songs written about cowboys. Read the poetry inspired by Dr. Higley below to learn about some famous Kansas inventions.

WHO INVENTED EACH OF THE ITEMS BELOW?
Read the limericks for clues and write the inventors' names below the illustrations.

Invention 1
Omar Knedlik, in ol' Coffeyville,
Wanted a drink with a little more thrill.
The drink he awaited
Was well carbonated
And came with a very nice chill.

Invention 2
Last name Naismith, first name James
Was bored of all the normal games.
Then came his sport
With one ball and a court:
Into baskets the players all aim.

Invention 3
A smart, clever man known as William J. Purvis
Built a machine with a really great purpose.
Its wings spin around,
It lands flat on the ground,
It flies high and provides a great service.

Invention 4
Mike Miller was in the eighth grade.
He ate pizza a great chef had made,
But his lousy utensil
Snapped just like a pencil;
So he made a new fork with a blade.

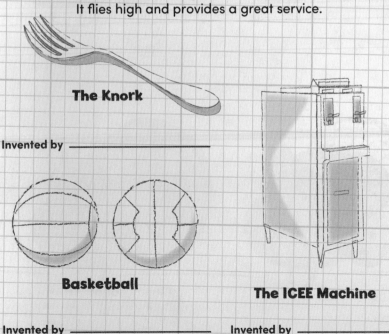

The Knork

Invented by _____

Basketball

Invented by _____

The ICEE Machine

Invented by _____

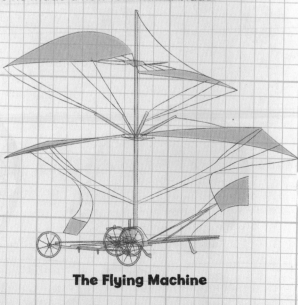

The Flying Machine

Invented by _____

THE KANSAS COSMOSPHERE

is one of the world's largest space museums. Inside, visitors can see rockets, a spacecraft recovered from the bottom of the Atlantic Ocean, and the world's fastest spy plane. Secret agents who fly spy planes sometimes use codes called ciphers. A cipher replaces each letter of the alphabet with a symbol. Use the cipher provided to learn more about the artifacts in the Cosmosphere.

CIPHER CHARTS

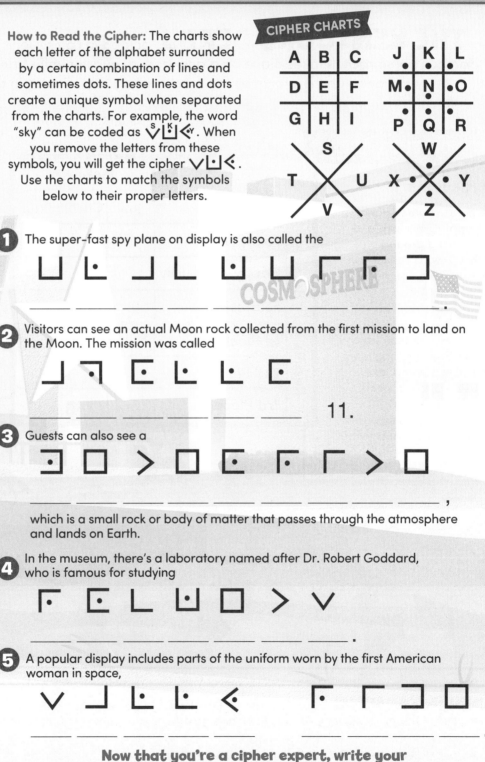

How to Read the Cipher: The charts show each letter of the alphabet surrounded by a certain combination of lines and sometimes dots. These lines and dots create a unique symbol when separated from the charts. For example, the word "sky" can be coded as ⱽ⎣ᴷ⎦⟨ʸ. When you remove the letters from these symbols, you will get the cipher ∨⎣·⎦⟨. Use the charts to match the symbols below to their proper letters.

1 The super-fast spy plane on display is also called the

_____ _____ _____ _____ _____ _____ _____ _____ _____ .

2 Visitors can see an actual Moon rock collected from the first mission to land on the Moon. The mission was called

_____ _____ _____ _____ _____ _____ 11.

3 Guests can also see a

_____ _____ _____ _____ _____ _____ _____ _____ _____ ,

which is a small rock or body of matter that passes through the atmosphere and lands on Earth.

4 In the museum, there's a laboratory named after Dr. Robert Goddard, who is famous for studying

_____ _____ _____ _____ _____ _____ _____ .

5 A popular display includes parts of the uniform worn by the first American woman in space,

_____ _____ _____ _____ _____ _____ _____ _____ _____ .

Now that you're a cipher expert, write your name using the symbols from the cipher charts!

33

KENTUCKY
✳ The Bluegrass State ✳

Capital: **Frankfort** ✳ Abbreviation: **KY**
15th State: **Joined June 1, 1792**

THE KENTUCKY DERBY, located in Louisville, is Kentucky's most famous horse race. It takes place on a one-and-a-quarter-mile track called Churchill Downs and is known as the most exciting two minutes in sports.

WHO WON THE RACE?

Instructions

Three horses named Fancy Feet, Happy-Go-Lucky, and Fearless raced around Churchill Downs. The jockeys in the race were named Jim, Carol, and Paul.

Using the clues, figure out which jockey raced on which horse and which racing team came in first, second, and third. Use the process of elimination and draw "x" marks in the chart's incorrect boxes and check marks in the correct boxes.

Answers		Jockeys		
		Jim	Carol	Paul
Horses	Fancy Feet			
	Happy-Go-Lucky			
	Fearless			
Results	1st Place			
	2nd Place			
	3rd Place			

Clues

- Jim didn't win the race and also didn't ride a horse whose name starts with the letter "F."
- Paul did not come in second place.
- Carol rode a horse with a two-word name. She finished the race after Jim.

HIDDEN IN THE HATS!
Some spectators at the Kentucky Derby wear bright colors and wild, elaborate hats. Circle the letters hidden in the hats. Rewrite the letters as they appear, from left to right, to complete the sentence below.

The fireworks show that kicks off the Kentucky Derby is called ____ ____ ____ ____ ____ ____ ____ Over Louisville.

34

WILDERNESS ROAD

Trailblazer and frontiersman Daniel Boone played a big part in the early settlement of Kentucky. In 1775, Boone and 30 men axed their way through difficult terrain to create a trail called the Wilderness Road. This trail led to some of the first settlements west of the Appalachian Mountains, including one named after Boone himself, Boonesborough.

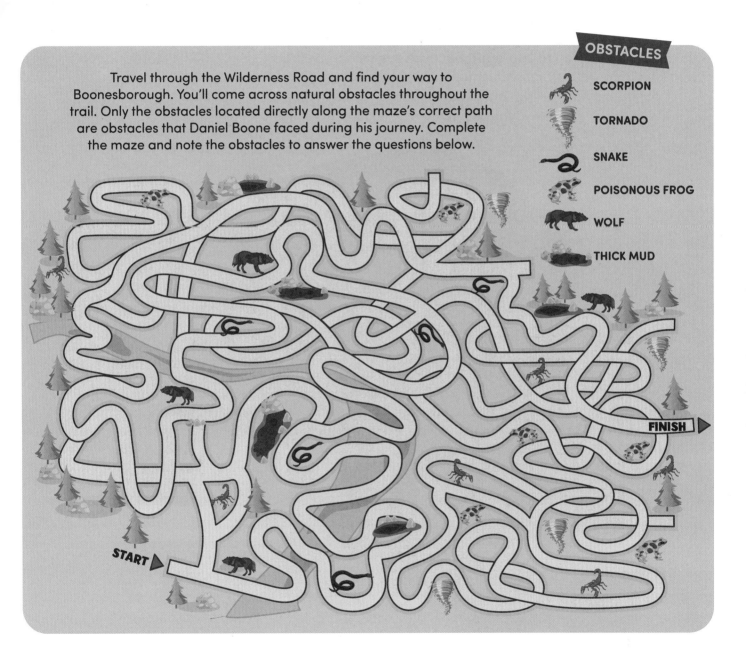

Travel through the Wilderness Road and find your way to Boonesborough. You'll come across natural obstacles throughout the trail. Only the obstacles located directly along the maze's correct path are obstacles that Daniel Boone faced during his journey. Complete the maze and note the obstacles to answer the questions below.

OBSTACLES
- SCORPION
- TORNADO
- SNAKE
- POISONOUS FROG
- WOLF
- THICK MUD

START ▶

FINISH ▶

Fun Fact

How many different types of obstacles did you come across? _____

Determine if this number is even or odd to read a fact about Wilderness Road.

Even: One of the main reasons why Daniel Boone forged the trail was to investigate rumors of gold in the area.

Odd: Settlers used salt from deposits found in the Kentucky territory to dry and preserve their food. (Removing moisture from food prevents bacteria growth.)

LOUISIANA
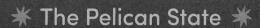
✳ The Pelican State ✳

Capital: **Baton Rouge** ✳ Abbreviation: **LA**
18th State: **Joined April 30, 1812**

SPORTSMAN'S PARADISE

is a nickname given to Louisiana because it is so well known for its outdoor adventures. People visit for the fishing, hiking, barbecuing, and bird-watching.

NAME THAT BIRD!
Use the bird clues to correctly label the birds in Sportsman's Paradise.

The **American coot** looks and behaves like a duck. It can be identified by its white bill.

The **red-headed woodpecker** uses its beak to chip at trees for food. It's known for its vibrant red head feathers.

A bird of Mexico, the **vermilion flycatcher** also has vibrant red-orange feathers. You can see them on its chest and can recognize the bird by the black markings around its eyes.

LOUISIANA BIRD CLUES!

The **wood duck** nests in hollow trees and is known for its vibrant colors.

The **brown pelican** is also known for its beak, which includes a large pouch on the underside of the bill.

 Did You Know? Fishing is a popular sport in Louisiana. Competitions are held throughout the state. These competitions are called fishing rodeos, and competitors fish for bass, catfish, trout, and more!

NEW ORLEANS & JAZZ

New Orleans clubs play music almost every night, but you don't have to go indoors to be entertained. In NoLa (a nickname for New Orleans), brass band parades fill the streets with music every Sunday. Neighbors join the parade, walking behind the band.

The musicians are called the "main line" or the "first line," and the people who follow are called the "second line." It's a weekly march of music and joy.

Musicians play saxophones, trumpets, drums, and trombones and parade throughout town.

Let's Draw!

Draw your very own jazz band!

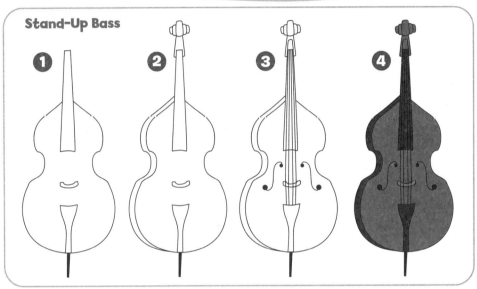

Stand-Up Bass

① ② ③ ④

Trombone

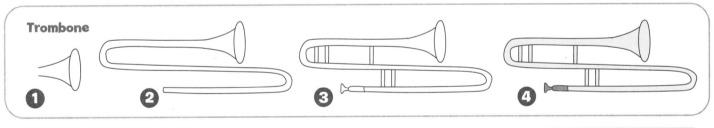

① ② ③ ④

Trumpet

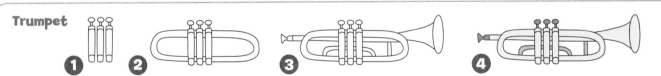

① ② ③ ④

Drum

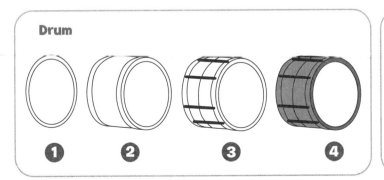

① ② ③ ④

Saxophone

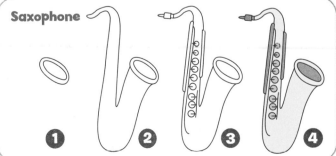

① ② ③ ④

MAINE
The Pine Tree State

Capital: **Augusta** * Abbreviation: **ME**
23rd State: **Joined March 15, 1820**

SAILING KNOTS

Sailing is a popular sport in Maine. Ropes (called "lines" in sailing) are used for many different purposes on a sailboat. Practice on a small piece of rope or some string to learn a few basic knots for controlling lines.

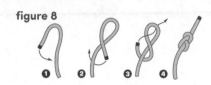

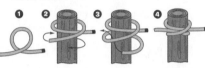

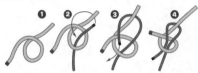

SAILBOAT DIAGRAM

Many different types of boats can often be seen sailing along Maine's coast. Read the diagram to learn some of the parts of a sailboat.

Large sailing ships called windjammers were designed as cargo ships in the 19th century. Today, windjammers are popular for sailing adventures.

Mast
Tall post carrying sails

Mainsail
Primary sail that moves the boat along

Boom
Rod holding the bottom of the mainsail

Tiller
Handle that controls the rudder

Jib
Triangular sail attached to the bow

Bow
Front part of the boat

Hull
Bottom part of the boat

Fender
Bumper to protect the sides of the boat from the dock

Rudder
Steering blade

Keel
Weighted blade that keeps the boat from tipping over on its side

SHIPWRECK SCAVENGER HUNT

Compass
Pearl necklace
Glass bottle
Captain's wheel
Silver utensils
Seashells
Treasure chest
Anchor
Starfish
Map

MORE THAN 1,300 SHIPS HAVE SUNK

off the coast of Maine in the last few centuries. Maine's rocky shores and violent weather lead many ships off their courses. Most shipwrecks are left in the ocean because it is too expensive to pull them out.

Let's Draw!

Maine has the second-largest moose population in the USA. (Alaska has the largest.) Draw your very own moose on a piece of paper!

1
2
3
4
5
6
7
8

MARYLAND

✳ The Old Line State ✳

Capital: **Annapolis** ✳ Abbreviation: **MD**
7th State: **Joined April 28, 1788**

BEAUTIFUL CHINCOTEAGUE HORSES live on Assateague

Island, which spans Maryland and Virginia. No one knows for sure how these feral horses (domesticated horses returned to the wild) ended up on the island. Legend has it that they arrived on a pirate ship or survived a shipwreck many centuries ago.

Many people call Chincoteague horses "ponies" because they are shorter than regular horses.
FIND AND CIRCLE 10 DIFFERENCES between the two Chincoteague horses.

Let's Draw!

The blue crab is the official Maryland state crustacean, and the crab industry plays an important part in the state economy. Maryland blue crabs are known all over the USA. The Chesapeake Bay is the most popular place for crabbing.

1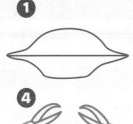

2

3

4

5

6

40

APPLES TO APPLES

Apple cider has been part of Maryland's history since the 1600s. That's right! Apples and pears were planted throughout the state hundreds of years ago and are still made into delicious drinks today.

Find and circle the ten rows of four matching apples in the grid below. Hint: The rows can be horizontal, vertical, or diagonal.

MASSACHUSETTS

✸ The Bay State ✸

Capital: **Boston** ✸ Abbreviation: **MA**
6th State: **Joined February 6, 1788**

THE WAMPANOAG NATIVE AMERICAN TRIBE

lived in Plymouth far before
the Pilgrims arrived in the 1600s.

WAMPANOAG WORD SEARCH

Learn some words from the Wampanoag's native language. Find the listed words below in the word search. The English translation of each word will cross through its Wampanoag counterpart in the word search.

Sannup ____ ____ ____

Squaw ____ ____ ____ ____ ____

Cone ____ ____ ____

Mishoon ____ ____ ____ ____

Wetu ____ ____ ____ ____

Wobsacuck ____ ____ ____ ____ ____

Ausupp ____ ____ ____ ____ ____ ____

Nitchicke ____ ____ ____ ____

```
R  A  I  T  M  O  Y  C  R  N
A  U  S  U  P  P  B  O  U  I
C  R  F  S  B  S  U  N  M  T
C  E  X  H  Q  R  X  E  K  C
O  T  I  T  R  U  D  N  A  H
O  U  P  A  D  R  A  B  F  I
N  N  C  N  A  M  O  W  B  C
G  O  R  F  B  B  A  W  L  K
O  K  O  Z  W  W  Z  O  Z  E
G  U  A  F  B  L  U  B  X  O
T  Q  O  H  B  P  L  S  E  C
A  U  T  G  U  N  Z  A  M  K
W  A  A  N  R  J  G  C  I  U
M  S  N  E  C  L  R  U  S  Q
R  A  L  S  E  O  H  C  H  N
S  S  N  W  V  Q  V  K  O  N
C  R  F  S  E  K  T  A  O  B
P  A  N  O  D  T  H  P  N  D
Y  L  C  R  H  O  U  S  E  I
```

Did You Know?

The old style spelling of Plymouth was Plimoth.

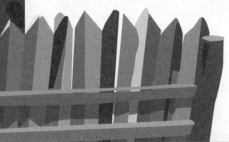

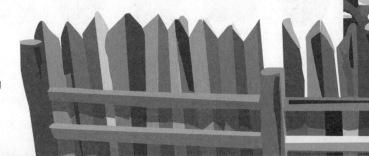

GAME OF HUBBUB

When the Pilgrims arrived in America, they learned about the traditions of the Wampanoag people. One of these traditions was the game of Hubbub, also known as the Bowl Game. It is a two-person game that relies on mathematics and chance. Follow the instructions to play this game with a friend.

MATERIALS

☐ 5 large buttons ☐ Black permanent marker ☐ Small bowl ☐ 50 toothpicks

MAKE YOUR GAME PIECES

1 Use the permanent marker to draw stars on the flat side of two of the buttons. Leave the other sides of these buttons blank.

2 Draw X's on the flat sides of the other three buttons. Leave the other sides of these buttons blank as well. These five buttons will act as your two-sided dice.

HOW TO PLAY HUBBUB

Step 1: Sit across from your opponent.

Step 2: Place your buttons in the bowl and shake the bowl well in order to mix them up.

Step 3: Roll the buttons out of the bowl and onto a flat surface.

Step 4: Look at the combination of buttons you rolled. How many X's are showing? How many stars are showing? How many blank sides are showing? Look at the scoring guide to see if you earned any toothpicks.

Step 5: Now it's your opponent's turn to roll the buttons and try to earn some toothpicks. Each toothpick you or your opponent collect represents one point. When all the toothpicks are collected, the player with the most points wins the game!

Scoring Guide

5 blank sides up =	3 toothpicks
5 marked sides up =	8 toothpicks
4 marked sides up =	1 toothpick
2 stars and 3 blanks =	3 toothpicks
3 X's and 2 blanks =	3 toothpicks
Other combinations =	0 toothpicks

Fun Fact

Wampanoag players would chant the sound "hub" over and over again to try to distract their opponents while they rolled the dice. This is where the game gets its name!

MICHIGAN
✳ The Wolverine State ✳

Capital: **Lansing** ✳ Abbreviation: **MI**
26ᵗʰ State: **Joined January 26, 1837**

SYMBOLS & LANDMARKS OF MICHIGAN

Many images can come to mind when thinking of the Wolverine State: winter weather, the waters of the Great Lakes, cars and the auto industry, and more!

Use the illustrations in each clue to fill in the crossword puzzle and learn more about the symbols and landmarks of Michigan.

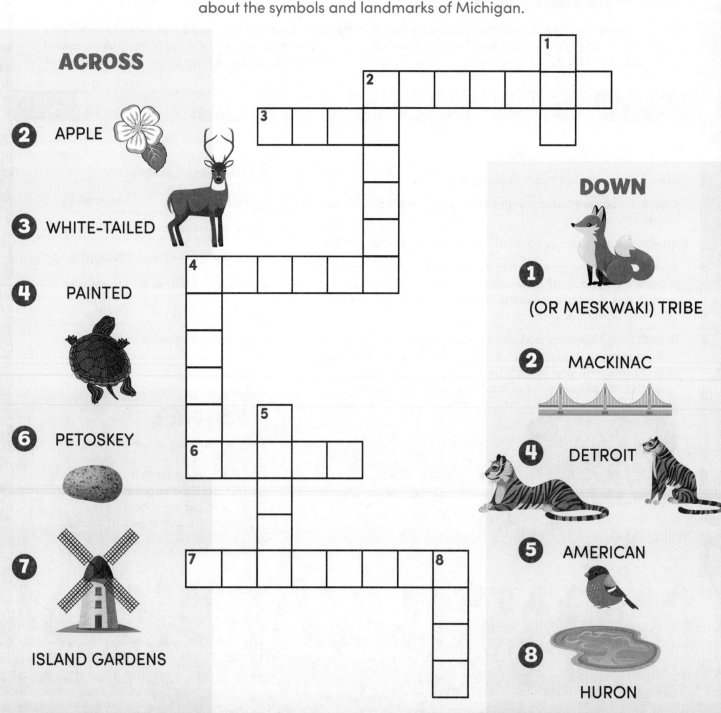

ACROSS

2 APPLE

3 WHITE-TAILED

4 PAINTED

6 PETOSKEY

7 ISLAND GARDENS

DOWN

1 (OR MESKWAKI) TRIBE

2 MACKINAC

4 DETROIT

5 AMERICAN

8 HURON

MICHIGAN BINGO

Michigan is full of sights, attractions, and curiosities of all kinds. Fill out the bingo card to explore fun things to do in the mitten-shaped state.

Draw an X through a box if it describes an activity you've done. See if your activities create any up-and-down, side-to-side, or corner-to-corner rows! Circle the activities you want to try.

DRAW A DINO	VISIT A FESTIVAL	SWIM IN A SPRING	USE A TELESCOPE	VISIT A GARDEN
Dinosaur Gardens Prehistoric Zoo	The Tulip Time Festival	Kitch-iti-kipi (Freshwater Spring)	James C. Veen Observatory	Matthaei Botanical Gardens
EAT ICE CREAM	**BROWSE A BOOKSTORE**	**LOOK AT A MURAL**	**FEED SOME FISH**	**GO HIKING**
Superman Ice Cream	John K. King Used and Rare Books	Diego Rivera's "Detroit Industry"	Belle Isle Aquarium	Porcupine Mountains Wilderness State Park
STUDY ROCK CARVINGS	**FIND A FOSSIL**	**FREE SPACE**	**LISTEN TO A BELL TOWER**	**TOUR A CASTLE**
Sanilac Petroglyphs	Petoskey State Park	★	Nancy Brown Peace Carillon	Curwood Castle
VISIT A HISTORIC TOWN	**CROSS A BRIDGE**	**SEE A LIGHTHOUSE**	**RIDE A ROLLER COASTER**	**LEARN HISTORY**
Mackinac Island	Ada Covered Bridge	Point Iroquois Lighthouse	Shivering Timbers Wooden Roller Coaster	Michigan History Center
CLIMB A SAND DUNE	**SWIM IN A LAKE**	**PLAY A GAME**	**WATCH A REENACTMENT**	**GO TO THE BEACH**
Sleeping Bear Dunes National Lakeshore	Lake Superior	Mid-Michigan Children's Museum	Fort Mackinac	Holland State Park Beach

MINNESOTA

✳ The Land of 10,000 Lakes ✳

Capital: **Saint Paul** ✳ Abbreviation: **MN**
32nd State: **Joined May 11, 1858**

THE OJIBWE NATIVE AMERICAN people (also called the Chippewa in some regions) have lived in present-day Minnesota since the fifth century, when, according to stories passed down through generations, tribe leaders received a prophecy to travel west to "the land where food grows on water."

DECODE THE PROPHECY! Cross out the letters marked with odd numbers.
Read what's remaining to learn what some believe the legend to have meant.

7 28634 96 1208 423 9 64 821 02685 4 7 620432
SWILFD TRCICE ISA QAN AQBUATIUC OGRASVS

1 496528 2306 84 0721 44 890 6128 47238 4
HTCHIAT GBROWS BGEDST IDN SFHALELZOW

72 564290 5 072623 6180 541 262 69143 40
YWGATEAR. BWEHEND TFHE XPHROPHKHEWCY

49262108 4 76 212704 852 4 6 10892 634
SNPEARKS OWF FJOZOD GIROWVINAG OYN

678204 7 81628 9 4 1025462 6 812 904 5 21 483026
WTATER, KMXANY MBCELKIEVE TLHCIS HRNEFJERS

634 9 62850 7 04162 4 9 62452 0182 302964
TAO PWILSD ORISCE, WGHICTH HUAS VBENEN

4 220586265 3 8 1492 6 124367 26 27 4 1282067498
HARVLESTEDWD XBZY NUATBIAVE AHMCERICAFNGS

562 1 228 9 260127 24 1058 2 32 7 6290 2 264 1 25
AIN PMINONESKOETA AFQOR LCMENRTURIEMSP.

46

Minnesota is known for its **FREEZING WINTERS**. Literally! The Land of 10,000 Lakes receives more snow each year than most other states in America.

HAVE SOME CHILLY FUN! Find and circle the words carved into the ice to learn some of the popular winter activities in Minnesota.

SNOWMOBILING

ICE FISHING

SKIING

MAKING SNOW ANGELS

SNOWBALL FIGHTS

SNOWSHOEING

ICE SKATING

MISSISSIPPI

✳ The Magnolia State ✳

Capital: Jackson ✳ **Abbreviation: MS**
20th State: Joined December 10, 1817

ALLIGATORS IN MISSISSIPPI

There are many alligators in Mississippi's rivers and swamps. In the daytime, it can be difficult to see them on the shore. Lying underneath the trees, they blend in with the grass and mud.

Fun Facts

The alligator is the official Mississippi state reptile. It can grow up to 15 feet long and weighs up to 1,000 pounds. The alligator species is believed to be 150 million years old!

Let's Draw!

Draw your own alligator on a blank piece of paper!

 1
 2

3
4

5
6

THE MAGNOLIA

became the official state tree of Mississippi in 1938 after the director of forestry held an "election" among Mississippi school children. The students chose the magnolia tree in a landslide, outvoting the oak tree, pine tree, and dogwood tree.

Thirty-five years before, thousands of school children also voted to select the magnolia blossom to be the Mississippi state flower.

CIRCLE THE ROWS OF THREE MAGNOLIAS among the other flowers. The total number of circled rows will tell you how many votes were cast for the magnolia blossom!

2 rows = 5,906 votes

4 rows = 12,745 votes

6 rows = 24,200 votes

8 rows = 2,405 votes

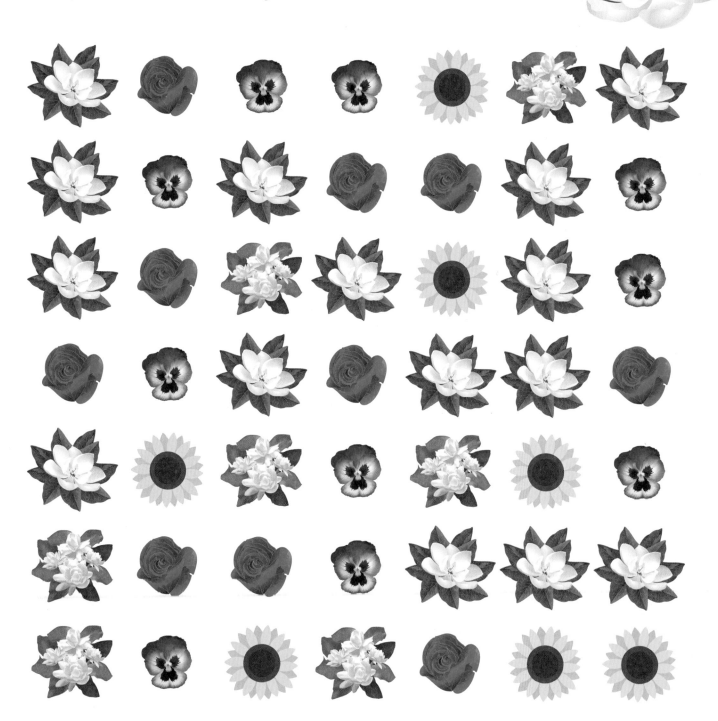

MISSOURI
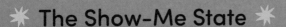
✳ The Show-Me State ✳

Capital: **Jefferson City** ✳ Abbreviation: **MO**
24th State: **Joined August 10, 1821**

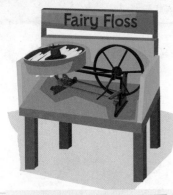

THE 1904 WORLD'S FAIR in St. Louis
revealed innovative inventions, like the telegraph, and introduced new foods, like hot dogs in buns, iced tea, and cotton candy (nicknamed "fairy floss").

TRANSLATE THE MESSAGE
Use the Morse code alphabet to decode the message below.

Morse Code Alphabet

A	·—	S	···
B	—···	T	—
C	—·—·	U	··—
D	—··	V	···—
E	·	W	·——
F	··—·	X	—··—
G	——·	Y	—·——
H	····	Z	——··
I	··	0	—————
J	·———	1	·————
K	—·—	2	··———
L	·—··	3	···——
M	——	4	····—
N	—·	5	·····
O	———	6	—····
P	·——·	7	——···
Q	——·—	8	———··
R	·—·	9	————·
Period	·—·—·—		
Comma	——··——		

TELEGRAPH operators used a special alphabet called
Morse code to send and receive messages through the radio in the early 1900s. Each dot represents a short tap of the telegraph button. Each dash represents a long tap of the button (three times as long as a short tap).

B T W O A P P C I Y T D
M Q A N O C G C F U N N E L C L O U D I U T
H T T G R U D C Q J X F C R S A U N T F
E O M V N P A E K F W L Y H U N W A P A
K F S R O C A R B S X U D O M E P D J K
I D N S O D B V S J J E W T B E S E H
C A P L O V X O Z I X J G E R P X R
N D H D W A I R S T R E A M C O T
F O E A A T U Y H A J T K H E U S M O B
F R I R R Z C X S I S Q U L T E
A I R N W A L L C L O U D L
L M C F I A D O A A P N T Y O
E I P U N T H U J L L S D
L R N G E W D C E J O
Y E N A R H S C
G S E U S Y X L
U L S L J P M F
P T N U B A O A
O G R C J U N
R T E X D U
B N A K C Q X T
V A M U T N
Q D J X W
H B O E I
R O P E
P Y O C

Missouri is known for its
EXTREME CLIMATE
due to its location in the middle of the USA.

Without any large mountains to shield the state from strong wind currents, cold air from the Arctic and warm air from the Gulf of Mexico often meet in Missouri. These conditions can produce tornadoes, which are common in Missouri in the spring.

MISSOURI WORD TWISTER
Find hidden tornado terms in this word twister.

Accessory Clouds small clouds attached to a larger cloud system

Airstream air flowing in the same circulation

Atmospheric Pressure the force exerted on a surface by the weight of the air above it

Cold-air Funnel a weak tornado created by a small thunderstorm when the air is unusually cold

Fujita Scale a scale classifying tornado strength, F0 being the weakest and F5 being the strongest

Funnel Cloud a rotating column of air extending from the base of a thunderstorm (a funnel cloud becomes a tornado when it touches ground)

Inflow Jets streams of air near the ground flowing into the base of a tornado

Landspout a tornado that is not connected to a wall cloud

Rope a narrow funnel of air usually seen as a tornado dissipates

Supercell a severe storm that lasts for hours

Tornado a violently rotating column of air in contact with the ground

Tornado Family a group of tornadoes produced by one supercell

Tornado Warning a warning announced when a tornado is sighted

Wall Cloud a low-hanging accessory cloud attached to a larger cell

Waterspout a tornado that reaches a water surface

Capital: Helena ✳ **Abbreviation: MT**
41st State: Joined November 8, 1889

One of Montana's nicknames is the **TREASURE STATE** because of the many natural minerals found here, including copper, silver, and gold. One of the most beautiful Montana treasures is the Yogo sapphire. Found only in Montana, the Yogo sapphire is a precious gemstone known for its deep blue color.

GO ON A TREASURE HUNT and circle every Yogo sapphire on the page. When you're done, count how many you've circled to answer the question below.

Yogo sapphire

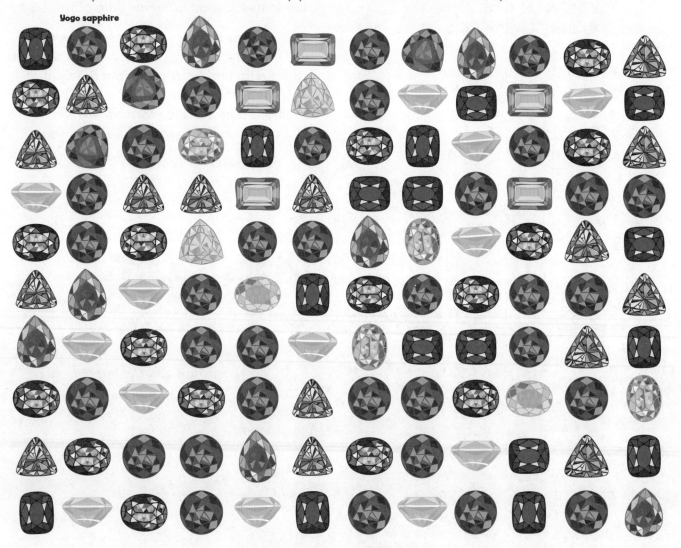

Montana's State Motto

How many Yogo sapphires did you count? Circle the number below to learn the English translation of Montana's state motto, "Oro y Plata."

35 "Gold and Silver"   **41** "Treasure for All"

49 "Search for Sapphires"   **52** "Land of Gems"

MONTANA DINOSAUR TRAIL

So many fossils have been discovered in Montana that the state has its own special route called the Montana Dinosaur Trail!

Fill in the blanks with the dinosaur names from the trail map.

Seismosaurus

Gryposaurus

Plesiosaur

Triceratops

Maiasaura

Tyrannosaurus rex

Hadrosaur

_ _ _ _ _ _ _ _ _ _ _ _ _
      4   5

_ _ _ _ _ _ _ _ _ _ _ _
7   6

_ _ _ _ _ _ _ _ _ _
     2

_ _ _ _ _ _ _ _ _ _ _
          9

_ _ _ _ _ _ _ _ _ _
10   11

_ _ _ _ _ _ _ _
1   3

_ _ _ _ _ _ _ _ _
       8

Once you've filled in all the names of the dinosaurs, write the numbered letters in their matching blanks to complete the phrase

The study of dinosaurs is called _ _ _ _ _ _ _ _ _ _ _
                              1 2 3 4 5 6 7 8 3 9 10 11

NEBRASKA
The Cornhusker State

Capital: Lincoln ✳ **Abbreviation: NE**
37th State: **Joined March 1, 1867**

THE SIOUX, CHEYENNE, AND PAWNEE

have called Nebraska home for ages. Native American culture is an irreplaceable part of the state's history. Some of Nebraska's towns, cities, and villages are named after Native American words!

WORD SCRAMBLE Unscramble the letters to uncover the Native American meaning of each of these Nebraskan places. Write the unscrambled translations in the blank spaces. Use the illustrations as clues!

Monowi
Fwloer

_ _ _ _ _ _

Niobrara
Riunngn
Wtaer

_ _ _ _ _ _ _

_ _ _ _ _

Nebraska
Ftal
Weatr

_ _ _ _

_ _ _ _ _

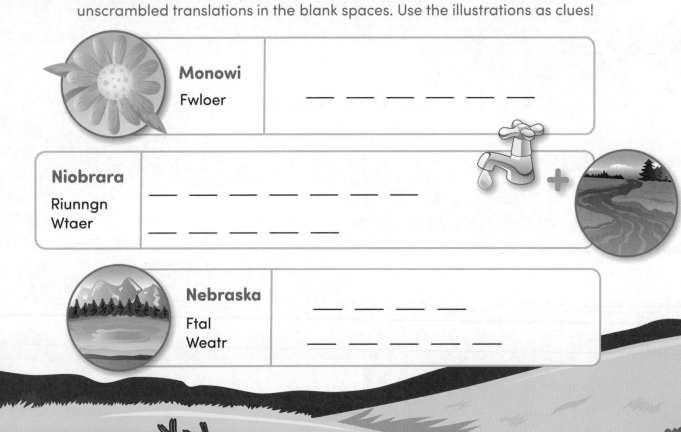

A RABBIT WITH ANTLERS?

The jackalope is an antlered species of rabbit rumored to live in the Nebraska plains. People still claim to see the jackalope, even though the creature is mythical.

BLACK-TAILED PRAIRIE DOGS are the only
species of prairie dogs native to Nebraska. They are burrowing animals
that dig underground for shelter, building homes for themselves
beneath the prairie lands of the Cornhusker State.

INTO THE BURROW! Start on the brown circle and count by **2s**
through the number maze to follow the prairie dog to its burrow.

2	4	6	8	16	15	55	56	30	52	19	51
4	10	8	42	65	2	13	18	54	26	23	7
12	32	10	12	14	16	18	20	22	24	97	92
21	20	11	87	54	83	78	23	76	26	27	161
21	74	91	44	42	40	38	65	60	28	86	34
67	11	33	46	84	14	36	34	32	30	42	125
88	10	51	48	78	53	85	67	14	54	63	17
44	54	52	50	52	74	76	78	80	82	84	55
39	56	58	64	95	72	62	74	85	84	86	92
55	58	66	46	52	70	72	76	85			
59	60	62	64	66	68	215	68	98			
85	70	62	66	15	75	86	96	80			

NEVADA
The Silver State

Capital: Carson City * **Abbreviation: NV**
36th **State: Joined October 31, 1864**

THE DESERT TORTOISE

is Nevada's state reptile and the largest reptile species in the Southwest. It can live for more than 70 years, spending most of its time in burrows. The tortoise has a domed shell that acts as camouflage and protection from predators.

The bird is believed to be one of the tortoise's ancestors!

```
I P L E U R A L S I
I Z O M T B D F M T P O M
D L C U K Y W N J A M B G A X
S L A A B O X L B P R D U N D M
D B L E N R O U G P Q N G S L O N Q
T D A I M A Y B I Z H U I P R Y U M
V A S R H P P L A S T R O N S O Y B
D R M B S Z A B G A M X J A P Q J E
U V F E R S C U T E D C H L T A N
L Q N T A M E R A N P K S S V F
B I L R L P E C T O R A L S
G W E U X F U L B P S
P V G U L F Y I
```

TORTOISE SHELL WORD SEARCH

CARAPACE top portion of shell that covers the tortoise's back

PLASTRON bottom portion of shell that covers the tortoise's stomach

SCUTE outer layer of rough "shields" (shaped segments) that protect the inner shell

GULAR SHIELD portion of shell that extends beneath the chin of male tortoises

MARGINALS shell segments along the outside edge (part of the scute)

VERTEBRALS shell segments forming a line down the center of the back (part of the scute)

PLEURALS shell segments in between the marginals and vertebrals (part of the scute)

PECTORALS bottom shell segments covering the tortoise's chest

SIZING UP NEVADA CITIES!
Carson City, Henderson, Las Vegas, and Reno are some of the largest cities in the state. Read each city's description and remember the symbol next to each photo. Then solve these symbol puzzles to find out which city is the largest.

Las Vegas is known as the Entertainment Capital of the World. It has many unique hotels featuring famous landmark replicas, including the Statue of Liberty, the Eiffel Tower, and the Egyptian pyramids.

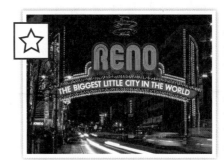

Reno is nicknamed the the Biggest Little City in the World. Set at the foot of the Sierra Nevada, Reno's skies are sunny for most of the year. Lake Tahoe, with its world-famous ski resorts, is only a 45-minute drive away.

Carson City was once known as America's smallest capital, given its small population. Only a few thousand people lived in Carson City when it became the state capital in 1864.

Henderson is located in the Mojave Desert. Inspired by the architecture of Las Vegas, Henderson built an apartment complex to look like a famous bridge in Italy.

Example

Every column must contain each of these city symbols: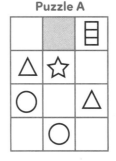

These symbols must appear only once in each row and column.

Puzzle A

Puzzle A Solution

Puzzle B

Puzzle C

Puzzle D

WHICH CITY IS THE LARGEST?
When you fill in the different puzzles, use the symbols from the shaded squares to list the cities in order from the smallest to largest.

A ___△___ Carson City   B _____   C _____   D _____

NEW HAMPSHIRE
✳ The Granite State ✳

Capital: **Concord** ✳ Abbreviation: NH
9th State: **Joined June 21, 1788**

LEAF PEEPING

Every fall, New Hampshire's forests display vibrant, deep colors as tree leaves change colors with the arrival of the new season. The forests attract tourists known as leaf peepers.

FALL FRACTIONS!

The top number of a fraction, called the **numerator**, represents the number of items within a group. The bottom number of a fraction, called the **denominator**, represents the total number of items within the group.

Example: The total number of maple leaves (your denominator) is 7. The number of yellow leaves (your numerator) is 3. How many leaves out of the entire group are yellow?

The answer is:
numerator
$$\frac{3}{7}$$
denominator

How many birch leaves are brown?

How many ash leaves are green?

How many oak leaves are yellow?

How many beech leaves are red?

MOUNT WASHINGTON, part of the White Mountains, is the tallest peak in New Hampshire and one of the snowiest places in the United States. It sees up to 23 feet of snow each year, which is about the height of four people standing on top of one another!

SPELL IT WITH SNOW! Use the image clues to write each snowy word or phrase.

WHITE MOUNTAIN NATIONAL FOREST

is an outdoor adventure destination loved by hikers, skiiers, picnickers, swimmers, and more!

Learn about some of the things you can find at the park by filling in the blanks. Write each letter from the top rows in the matching colored boxes beneath.

NEW JERSEY

The Garden State

Capital: Trenton ✳ **Abbreviation: NJ**
3rd State: Joined December 18, 1787

| Brook Trout | Eastern Goldfinch | Horse | Honeybee | Violet | Red Oak | Blueberry |

STATE SYMBOL SEARCH

Using the State Symbol Guide, circle three groups of State Creatures and three groups of State Plants in the puzzle. Make sure the groups that you circle match the State Symbol Guide exactly. The groups may appear vertically, horizontally, or diagonally.

STATE SYMBOL GUIDE

State Creatures   State Plants

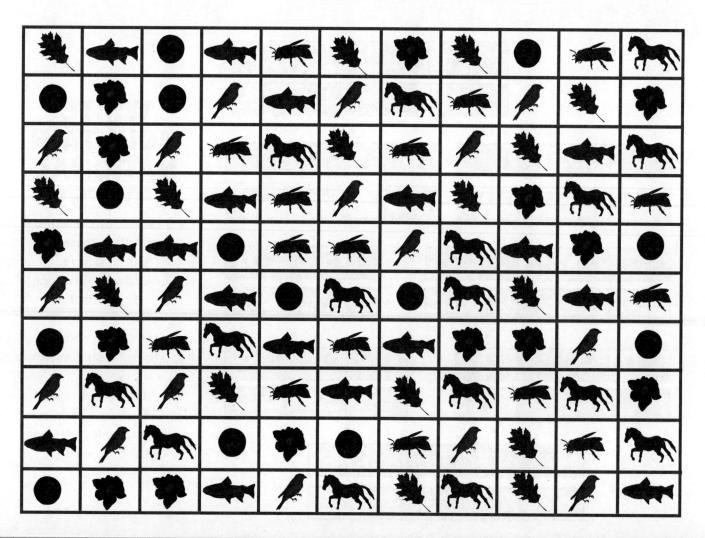

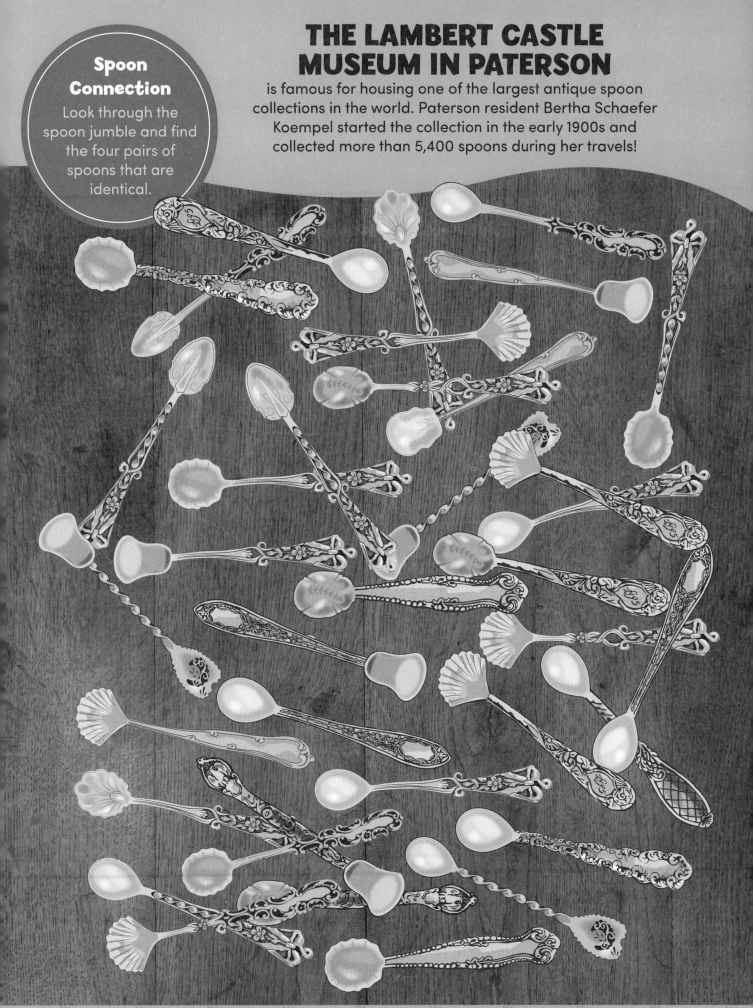

is famous for housing one of the largest antique spoon collections in the world. Paterson resident Bertha Schaefer Koempel started the collection in the early 1900s and collected more than 5,400 spoons during her travels!

Spoon Connection

Look through the spoon jumble and find the four pairs of spoons that are identical.

NEW MEXICO

✳ The Land of Enchantment ✳

Capital: **Santa Fe** ✳ Abbreviation: **NM**
47th State: **Joined January 6, 1912**

WHITE SANDS NATIONAL PARK covers about 275 square miles of southern New Mexico and northern Mexico. It receives more rain and has much colder winters than other North American deserts, making it home to some unique desert animals and plant life.

EXPLORE THE DESERT! Cross out the image that interrupts the pattern in each row to identify which plants and animals don't actually live in New Mexico's White Sands National Park.

BALLOON FIESTA!

The Albuquerque International Balloon Fiesta brings people together for nine days of colorful, sky-high fun every year. More than 500 hot-air balloons fill the sky with their vibrant colors as friends and family watch below.

Get Colorful! Use colored pencils, crayons, or markers to fill these hot-air balloons with your favorite hues.

NEW YORK

☀ The Empire State ☀

Capital: Albany ☀ **Abbreviation: NY**
11th State: Joined July 26, 1788

TOWER LIGHTS

Since 1976, the lights of the Empire State Building change color and display shapes to celebrate holidays and support charitable organizations.

For example, on Valentine's Day, the building's windows are illuminated red to create the symbol of a heart.

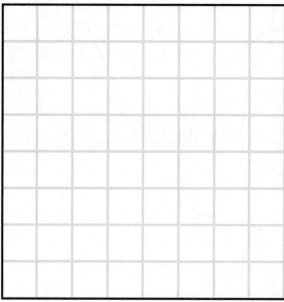

Use the Empire State Building as inspiration and color the "windows" in the grids to create your own symbols!

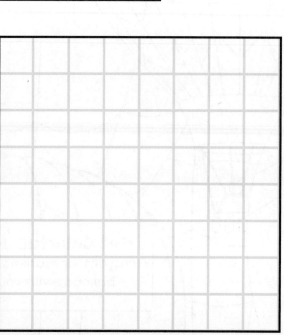

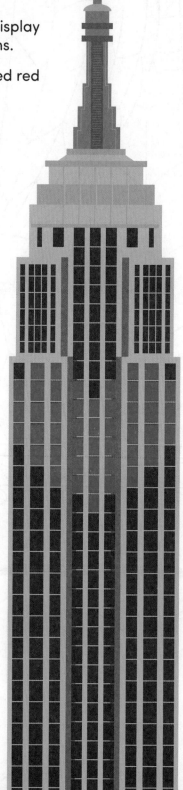

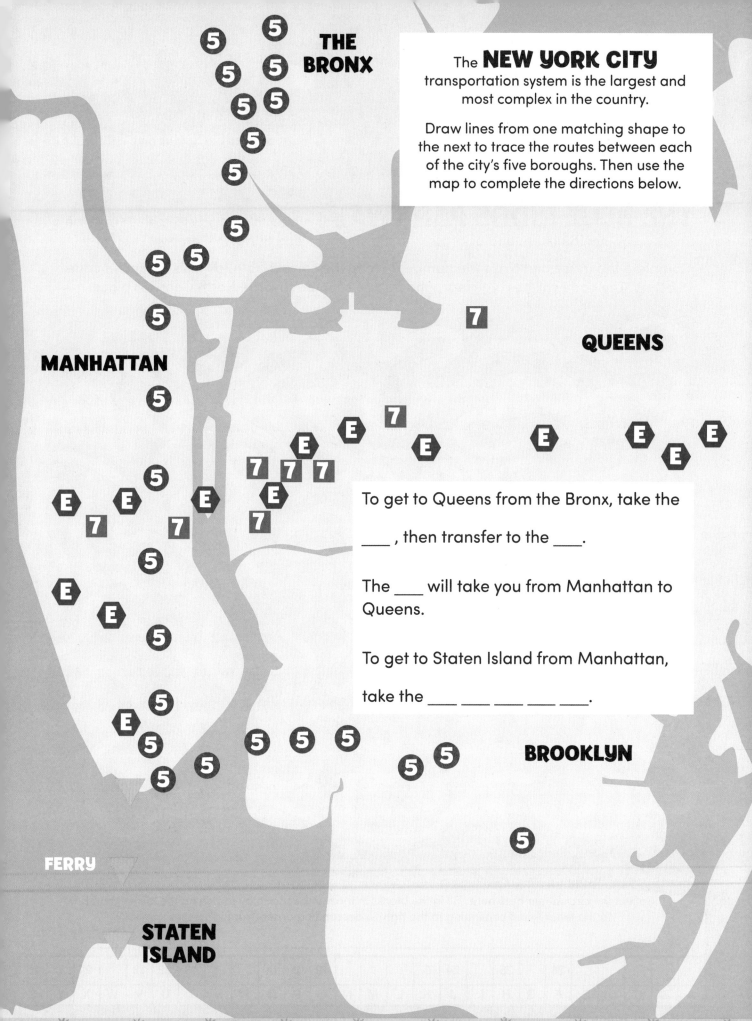

THE BRONX

The **NEW YORK CITY**

transportation system is the largest and most complex in the country.

Draw lines from one matching shape to the next to trace the routes between each of the city's five boroughs. Then use the map to complete the directions below.

QUEENS

MANHATTAN

To get to Queens from the Bronx, take the

___ , then transfer to the ___.

The ___ will take you from Manhattan to Queens.

To get to Staten Island from Manhattan,

take the ___ ___ ___ ___ ___.

BROOKLYN

FERRY

STATEN ISLAND

NORTH CAROLINA
❋ The Tar Heel State ❋

Capital: **Raleigh** ❋ Abbreviation: **NC**
12th State: **Joined November 21, 1789**

THE BLUE RIDGE PARKWAY is a beautiful road stretching from the northeastern end of Virginia to the southern end of North Carolina.

Complete the maze and circle the numbers along the correct path to finish the secret code below. The code will help you learn the names of some favorite North Carolina places.

SECRET CODE

Collect the circled numbers here. Fill in the blanks in the number code by matching the largest number to the letter A and continuing to the right in descending order (from largest to smallest).

_____ _____ _____ _____ _____ _____ _____ _____ _____ _____ _____ _____ _____ _____ _____ _____ _____ _____

A	B	C	D	E	F	G	H	I	J	K	L	M	N	O	P	Q	R	S	T	U	V	W	X	Y	Z
			25		26		24	9		1		19	2	14		4	18	22	13		21	7	15		

SECRET CODE SEARCH!

Match the numbers underneath the blanks to the letters in the secret code to learn the names of the North Carolina destinations below.

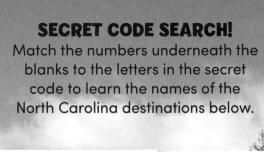

$\underline{\quad}$ $\underline{\quad}$ $\underline{\quad}$ $\underline{\quad}$ $\underline{\quad}$ $\underline{\quad}$ $\underline{\quad}$ $\underline{\quad}$ $\underline{\quad}$ $\underline{\quad}$ $\underline{\quad}$ $\underline{\quad}$ $\underline{\quad}$ $\underline{\quad}$
18   26   12   20   8   19   3   10   6   11   5   19   17   9

is a high cliff overlooking John's River Gorge. The cliff's name was inspired by the winds that blow around the rocks. If you throw something light off the cliff, like a fallen leaf, the winds often blow it back toward you.

$\underline{\quad}$ $\underline{\quad}$ $\underline{\quad}$ $\underline{\quad}$ $\underline{\quad}$ $\underline{\quad}$ $\underline{\quad}$ $\underline{\quad}$ $\underline{\quad}$ $\underline{\quad}$ $\underline{\quad}$ $\underline{\quad}$ $\underline{\quad}$
17   5   23   11   11   7   11   23   5   16   12   6   4

is a scenic spot on the Blue Ridge Parkway. Named after the Great Craggy Mountains, this stop attracts the most visitors in the summer when pink rhododendrons cover the mountain slopes.

$\underline{\quad}$ $\underline{\quad}$ $\underline{\quad}$ $\underline{\quad}$ $\underline{\quad}$ $\underline{\quad}$ $\underline{\quad}$ $\underline{\quad}$ $\underline{\quad}$ $\underline{\quad}$ $\underline{\quad}$
11   5   23   6   16   25   23   18   26   12   5

Mountain has beautiful lookouts and is connected to the Mile High Swinging Bridge. The Cherokee people originally named the mountain Tanawha (meaning "fabulous hawk"), and pioneers renamed it after recognizing what looked like a face of an old man in the cliffs.

$\underline{\quad}$ $\underline{\quad}$ $\underline{\quad}$ $\underline{\quad}$ $\underline{\quad}$ $\underline{\quad}$ $\underline{\quad}$ $\underline{\quad}$ $\underline{\quad}$ $\underline{\quad}$ $\underline{\quad}$
18   26   12   20   5   10   6   12   11   23   5

Cabin was built in the 1880s by a family of pioneers. Stepping inside the cabin and seeing household items preserved from the old days feels like you're stepping back in time.

$\underline{\quad}$ $\underline{\quad}$ $\underline{\quad}$ $\underline{\quad}$ $\underline{\quad}$ $\underline{\quad}$ $\underline{\quad}$ $\underline{\quad}$ $\underline{\quad}$ $\underline{\quad}$ $\underline{\quad}$ $\underline{\quad}$
8   19   19   9   10   6   11   11   8   23   4   4

Rock is a massive rock rising almost 4,000 feet in elevation in the Pisgah National Forest. When rainwater freezes on the rock's surface, the rock reflects the sun like a mirror. This effect inspired the rock's name.

NORTH DAKOTA
The Roughrider State

Capital: Bismarck ✳ **Abbreviation: ND**
39th State: Joined November 2, 1889

DINOSAUR FOSSILS WORD SEARCH

Many paleontologists go on trips to North Dakota searching for "dino mummies." Do some searching of your own and unearth the words below.

PALEONTOLOGIST a specialist who studies prehistoric life through fossils of plants and animals

MESOZOIC an era that took place between 250 million and 65 million years ago

EXTINCT a plant or animal that no longer exists

SKELETON a body frame made of bones

EVOLUTION a process during which organisms change over generations

HATCH to emerge from an egg

HERBIVORE an animal that eats only plants

CARNIVORE an animal that eats only meat

BONES hard white tissues that make up a skeleton

PREY animals hunted for food

```
E T U J U X E L O K H L K N N
N O B O N E S Z U C S U O F P
N L G I X M Y B T H V T Q C A
D X K R G E R A B R E F Z H L
S D Q G E S H E Y L R B I E E
Q U H U V O L E E X P G E R O
A H H E O Z P K U N L O Q B N
Z U T X L O S O T T G J P I T
K V K T U I G I H N R B F V O
T E V I T C I K F O O P V O L
C A R N I V O R E D V E T R O
H F S C O M R U W P P P L E G
I Q Y T N S W X L W R U H A I
P F K V M O A F A I E N U K S
L L H E V V L I C L Y I D R T
```

DINO DISCOVERY!

Before the Ice Age, herds of dinosaurs roamed the Badlands. In 1999, a teenager found a well-preserved mummy of a **hadrosaur**, a duck-billed dinosaur! It can be seen at the North Dakota Heritage Center in Bismarck.

BADLANDS NATIONAL PARK is a rugged area of the United
States known for its unusual rock formations, lack of water, and extreme temperatures. Bison, prairie dogs, and birds called black-billed magpies can all be spotted throughout this otherworldly park.

TURN BACK TIME! Learn how the Badlands got their name by filling the blanks with the letters on the clocks that match their listed times.

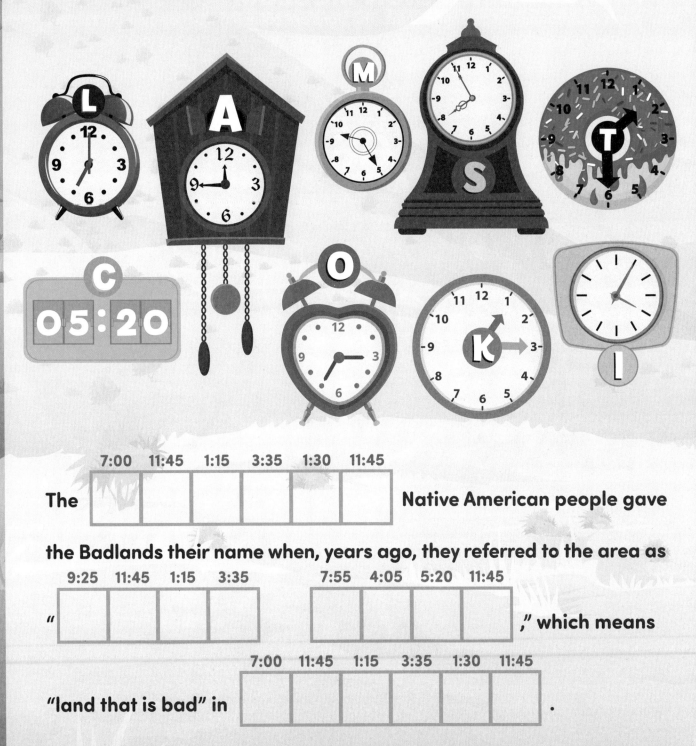

7:00	11:45	1:15	3:35	1:30	11:45

The ⬜⬜⬜⬜⬜⬜ Native American people gave

the Badlands their name when, years ago, they referred to the area as

9:25	11:45	1:15	3:35

7:55	4:05	5:20	11:45

" ⬜⬜⬜⬜ ⬜⬜⬜⬜ ," which means

7:00	11:45	1:15	3:35	1:30	11:45

"land that is bad" in ⬜⬜⬜⬜⬜⬜ .

OHIO

The Buckeye State

Capital: **Columbus** * Abbreviation: **OH**
17th State: **Joined March 1, 1803**

THE AMERICAN SIGN MUSEUM in Cincinnati is home to
hundreds of vintage road and shop signs. The signs are collected from all over the country
and help visitors imagine what American streets and roads used to look like.

There are many electric signs
preserved from as early as the
1900s, when it first became popular
to use signs illuminated with light
bulbs. Bright pink, green, and blue
signs light up the museum.

To learn Cincinnati's nickname, find and circle the hidden numbers in the scene.
Each number marks a letter from one of the signs. Fill in the blanks with the marked
letters by matching their numbers to the numbers below.

The ___ ___ ___ ___ ___ ___ ___ ___ ___
      1   2   3   4   5   6   7   8   9

SPACE EXPLORATION!
The Armstrong Air and Space Museum in Wapakonetta teaches visitors about Ohio-born astronauts Neil Armstrong and John Glenn. Armstrong was the first person to walk on the Moon. Glenn was the first American to orbit the Earth. Below is a picture of our planet taken from space!

Complete the puzzle by matching the four puzzle pieces to their empty spaces. Each correct match will answer a question about Ohio's famous astronauts.

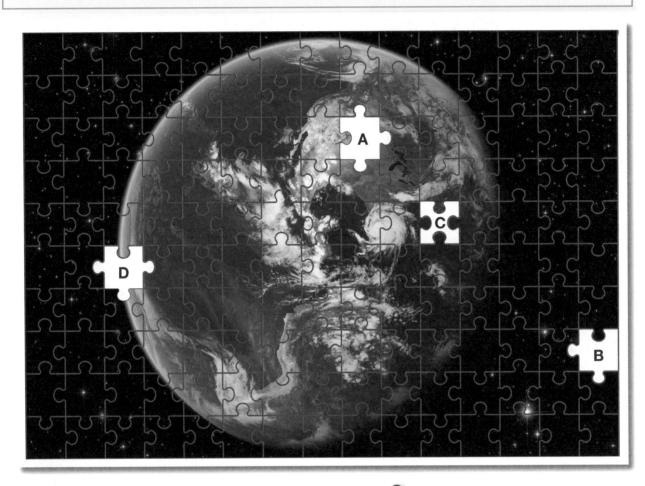

John Glenn traveled in space twice. After his second mission, at the age of _____, he became the oldest person to travel in space.

A. 65

B. 77

C. 80

D. 81

John Glenn was an experienced and brave pilot. In 1957, he set a speed record for flying from Los Angeles to New York in _____.

A. 1 hour and 54 minutes

B. 2 hours and 34 minutes

C. 3 hours and 23 minutes

D. 4 hours and 2 minutes

Neil Armstrong landed on the Moon in 1969. When he stepped off his spacecraft, his first words broadcast back to Earth were _____.

A. "That's one small step for man, one giant leap for mankind."

B. "The surface is fine and powdery."

C. "It's absolutely no trouble to walk around."

D. "It's quite dark here in the shadow and a little hard for me to see that I have good footing."

After retiring from NASA, Neil Armstrong became a _____.

A. politician

B. school teacher

C. pilot

D. university professor

OKLAHOMA
✳ The Sooner State ✳

Capital: Oklahoma City ✳ Abbreviation: **OK**
46th State: **Joined November 16, 1907**

Five of the 39 **INDIGENOUS TRIBES** that currently reside in the Sooner State lived in the area before the 1800s. Most were forced to relocate from their original homes to Oklahoma (which was then called "Indian Territory") after Congress passed the Indian Removal Act in 1830.

Today, indigenous people are more respectfully referred to as Native Americans. It's important to honor the culture and contributions of all tribes throughout the United States.

To learn the names of the five indigenous tribes native to Oklahoma, write each scrambled letter in the box beneath it that matches its color.

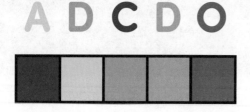

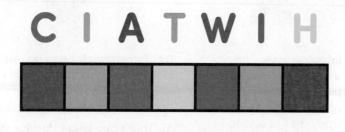

When Oklahoma's famous **DINOSAUR TRACKWAY** was first discovered in the 1980s, 47 types of dino tracks were found preserved in stone. Though erosion has since washed two-thirds of them away, the remaining prints tell us which massive dinosaurs once roamed Oklahoma's landscape.

Dino Connection!
Trace the lines below to connect each dinosaur species to its name and matching set of tracks.

Apatosaurus

Dimetrodon

Allosaurus

Saurophaganax

OREGON

✳ The Beaver State ✳

Capital: **Salem** ✳ Abbreviation: **OR**
33rd State: **Joined February 14, 1859**

THE WET WEST!

The Oregon coast is an amazing place. Some beaches are home to working ports and shipyards, and some are covered with rocks. Others are sloped with sand dunes.

Rock formations called "sea stacks" dot the Oregon coast. As you complete the maze, you'll come across 12 hidden letters. Write the letters in the order that you find them to learn the name of Oregon's most famous sea stack.

___ ___ ___ ___ ___ ___ ___ ___ ___ ___ ___ ___

THE SWALLOWTAIL BUTTERFLY

is Oregon's state insect. Scientists use gentle nets to collect butterflies like these for study. Swallowtails belong to the Papilionidae butterfly family, which can be found on every continent but Antarctica.

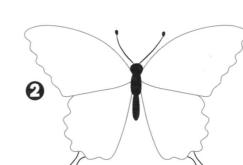

Let's Draw!

Draw your own family of swallowtail butterflies on a separate piece of paper.

①

②

③

④

Did You Know?

The swallow's forked tail is the inspiration for the butterfly's name.

①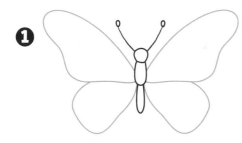

②

③

④

①

②

③

④

①

②

③

④

PENNSYLVANIA
✸ The Keystone State ✸

Capital: **Harrisburg** ✸ Abbreviation: **PA**
2nd State: **Joined December 12, 1787**

THE KEYSTONE STATE

A keystone is the center segment at the top of an arch that holds all the other pieces in place. Pennsylvania is called the Keystone State because it's located in the center of the USA's original 13 colonies.

Complete the math equations below and shade in the segments of the arch marked by the correct numbers. The correct pattern will reveal a fact about Pennsylvania.

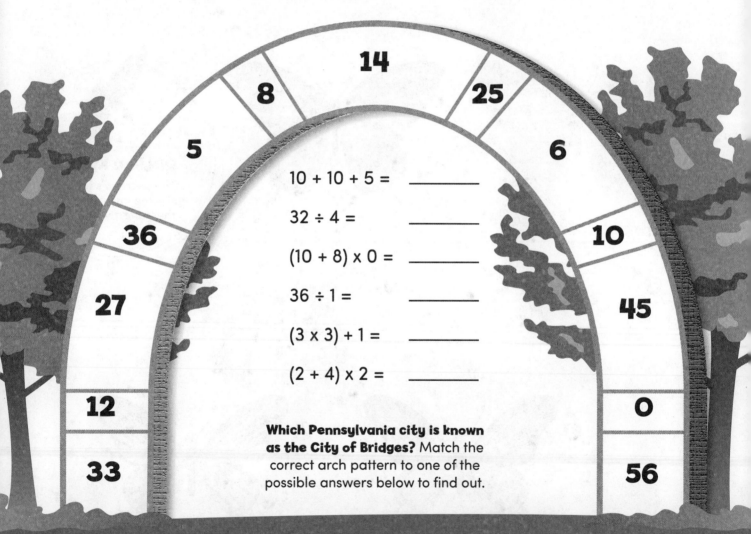

$10 + 10 + 5 =$ _____

$32 \div 4 =$ _____

$(10 + 8) \times 0 =$ _____

$36 \div 1 =$ _____

$(3 \times 3) + 1 =$ _____

$(2 + 4) \times 2 =$ _____

Which Pennsylvania city is known as the City of Bridges? Match the correct arch pattern to one of the possible answers below to find out.

Harrisburg

Pittsburgh

Philadelphia

Williamsport

76

HERSHEY, PENNSYLVANIA

Milton Hershey founded the Hershey Chocolate Company in 1894. You've probably heard Hershey's name before—his chocolate is sold all over the world. His hometown was renamed Hershey in his honor!

Find the hidden chocolate treats by completing the diagram below.

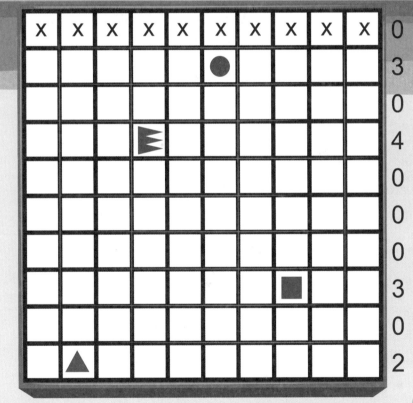

INSTRUCTIONS

This diagram represents a Hershey display table that features four chocolate treats. Find the exact locations of the treats in the diagram. Each treat is represented by a series of shapes.

Some shapes have already been filled in. The numbers along the sides of the diagram tell you the total number of shapes that belong in that row or column.

The chocolate treats can only be arranged horizontally, and no two treats sit directly next to each other.

Chocolate Bar :
2 Chocolate Kisses : ▲▲
3 Peanut Butter Cups : ●●●
Mini Chocolate Bar :

Hint: Start by "X"-ing out the squares you know are empty. For example, the top row contains 0 shapes, so all of the squares in this row get an "X".

Capital: Providence ✳ **Abbreviation: RI**
13th **State: Joined May 29, 1790**

Local **RHODE ISLAND VOCABULARY** is full of colorful slang for popular food and landmarks, and it's often spoken in a New England accent that's unique to the Ocean State.

Use the speech bubbles to help you circle the correct illustration for each of the Rhode Island words or phrases.

I'm craving something sweet. I could really go for a **cabinet** right now.

I'll have the **quahog** chowder, please!

Is there a **bubbler** around here? I'm parched!

Breakfast is almost ready. Where's the spatula? It's time to flip the **Johnny cakes**.

The **CRESCENT PARK CAROUSEL** in

Riverside, Rhode Island, was built in 1895 by Charles I.D. Looff and is a National Historic Landmark. Sixty-two hand-carved riding figures circle the center of the carousel, each one unique and special.

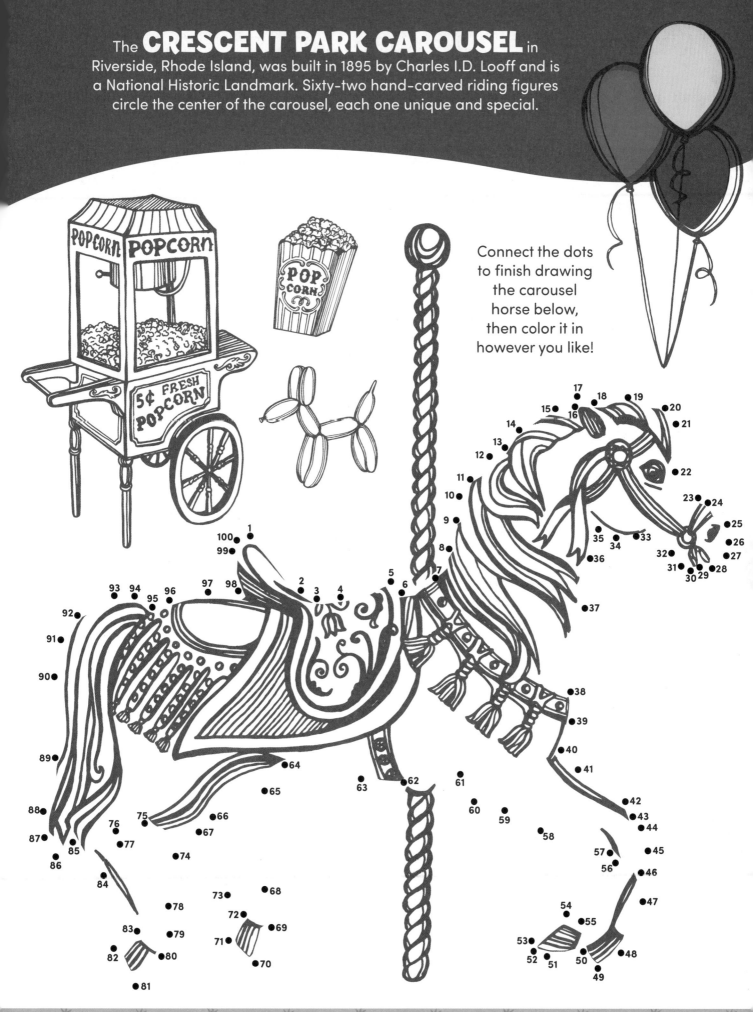

Connect the dots to finish drawing the carousel horse below, then color it in however you like!

SOUTH CAROLINA

✳ The Palmetto State ✳

Capital: **Columbia** ✳ Abbreviation: **SC**
8th State: **Joined May 23, 1788**

THE PALMETTO STATE isn't just full of seaside islands and historic buildings. There's plenty to explore throughout this gem of the south!

TIME TO PACK! Draw lines to connect each packed suitcase to its matching South Carolina activity.

Fishing at Caesars Head State Park

Stargazing at Dupont Planetarium

Swimming at Myrtle Beach

Taking Animal Photos at Riverbanks Zoo and Garden

South Carolina's state insect is called the
CAROLINA MANTID.
Its color ranges from dark brown to yellowish-green. This helps the mantid hide from predators and hunt for food.

Let's Draw!

Follow the steps below to draw your own mantid!

1 **2** **3** **4**

CAMOUFLAGE COLORS!
After you draw your first mantid, draw more with different camouflage colors! Camouflage is a technique designed to make something invisible in its environment. To hide in the woods, for example, wearing green or brown clothes would help you blend in with the trees.

Imagine your mantid on a tree branch. What colors would help it hide?

Capital: **Pierre** * Abbreviation: **SD**
40th State: **Joined November 2, 1889**

PALISADES STATE PARK may be the second-smallest park in South
Dakota, but the scenery is unforgettable. Split Rock Creek, which flows through the park, is
lined by rock formations made of billion-year-old Sioux quartzite.

Look closely at each disordered picture strip to find its correct place in the illustration.
Number each strip **1** through **4**, starting with the strip that should appear at the left.

The exterior of the **CORN PALACE** in Mitchell, South Dakota, is decorated with murals made of corn cobs every year.

Color the cobs marked with **even numbers yellow**, and color the cobs marked with **odd numbers brown** or **red**. The corn cobs will spell out the missing word to reveal South Dakota's state bird, which eats corn as part of its diet!

8	2	8	6	4	2	2	0	8	6
2	1	3	5	6	8	9	4	5	4
6	5	6	7	4	0	5	2	1	0
4	5	7	9	2	6	1	9	5	8
2	3	4	6	6	8	7	6	1	8
0	9	8	2	4	0	3	8	3	4
6	2	0	4	8	6	2	4	0	2
5	1	8	3	5	3	4	1	3	9
3	0	2	5	2	7	2	5	6	2
7	9	4	1	3	5	8	9	3	7
5	4	6	5	4	1	2	6	0	5
5	9	4	1	6	5	4	3	5	7
4	0	8	6	8	0	2	8	4	6
9	5	9	4	8	6	4	9	1	5
7	6	7	2	2	4	0	6	1	0
5	3	5	0	5	3	1	2	3	2
3	8	1	8	5	6	9	6	5	0
1	2	5	6	7	8	5	4	7	2
0	2	0	4	5	0	7	0	6	4
6	4	6	2	1	6	5	8	2	6
2	8	4	6	2	4	6	4	0	8

The South Dakota state bird is the **RING-NECKED** _____

TENNESSEE

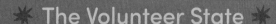

✳ The Volunteer State ✳

Capital: **Nashville** ✳ Abbreviation: **TN**
16th State: **Joined June 1, 1796**

NASHVILLE, TENNESSEE was the first city in the United States to receive an FM radio broadcasting license and has been a hotspot of the music industry ever since. It even earned the name **Music City** when radio host David Cobb first uttered the phrase over a broadcast in 1950. Today, Nashville still brings listeners music of all styles: country, gospel, rock n' roll, blues, bluegrass, southern gospel, and more!

MOVE TO THE BEAT! Start on the red circle and count by fives through the number maze to connect the tools to their instruments.

			8	105	25	30	35	40	52	11	55
			32	56	20	114	14	45	100	26	5
			5	10	15	110	177	50	234	15	96
15	20	19	54	216	48	74	195	55	36	200	146
105	95	90	85	80	75	70	65	60	64	86	34
85	100	43	59	184	14	61	105	55	74	24	125
59	105	118	300	73	100	37	67	0	213	63	19
66	110	115	120	125	130	140	14	54	110	111	87
97	94	150	87	95	135	62	45	112	125	45	33
165	160	155	150	145	140	99	76	85			
170	211	205	21	185	217	215	10	98			
175	180	185	190	195	200	205	210	215			

CAVE ANIMALS

Tennessee caves are full of animals, all of which belong to one of three groups: cave guests, cave lovers, and cave dwellers. **Cave guests**, such as bears, bats, and squirrels, use caves for shelter, nesting, or hibernation but can also live outside. **Cave lovers**, such as certain species of frogs and salamanders, prefer living inside caves and leave them only to find food. **Cave dwellers**, such as blind cave fish and cave crayfish, spend their entire lives inside caves.

GUIDE

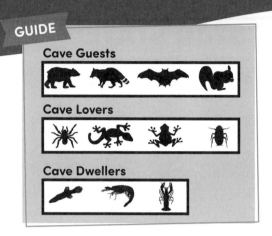

Cave Guests

Cave Lovers

Cave Dwellers

CAVE ANIMAL SEARCH!

In the puzzle below, one group appears once, one group appears twice, and one group appears three times.

Using the cave animals guide on the left, find and circle each group. Make sure you only circle the animal groups where each animal is featured in exactly the same order as shown in the guide.

The groups might appear horizontally, vertically, or diagonally. Have fun!

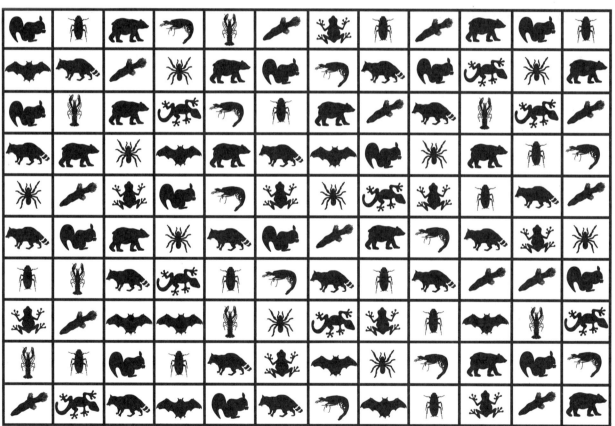

TROGLOFAUNA

How many groups of cave guests, cave lovers, and cave dwellers appear above? The correct answer will reveal the scientific name of each group.

1 group: _____ are called "troglobites."

2 groups: _____ are called "troglophiles."

3 groups: _____ are called "trogloxenes."

TEXAS
✳ The Lone Star State ✳

Capital: **Austin** ✳ Abbreviation: **TX**
28th State: **Joined December 29, 1845**

There's so much to say about **THE LONE STAR STATE!**
With rodeos, Route 66, world-famous food, and plenty of wide open spaces,
there's a lot to do and a lot to learn about Texas.

SORT THE SENTENCES! Draw lines to match each sentence to its correct
type on the right. Hint: Some sentences might match more than one type.

**Should I eat Tex-Mex
or Texas barbecue?**

**The first rodeo in the world took
place in Pecos, Texas, in 1883.**

Question

**Did you know Texas was the
28th state to join the union?**

Statement

Yeehaw!

Remember the Alamo!

Exclamation

Howdy, partner!

**The Texas flag shares its
colors with the American flag.**

Direction

Look at that armadillo!

THE CONGRESS AVENUE BRIDGE in Austin, Texas,
is home to quite an unexpected group of residents: Mexican free-tailed bats!
Every spring and summer, more than one million bats migrate to the bridge. It's
the largest urban bat colony in the United States! Visitors come from all around to
watch these flying creatures take flight at sunset, between **7:30 p.m.** and **8:30 p.m.**

TIME FOR FLIGHT! Look at the clocks above
and draw a check under each that shows a good
time to visit the bridge to see the bats.

UTAH
The Beehive State

Capital: **Salt Lake City** ✳ Abbreviation: **UT**
45th State: **Joined January 4, 1896**

SKIING IN UTAH

Look at the skis below and find the four skis that don't have a match. Unscramble the letters from those four unmatched skis to learn the name of a popular skiing spot.

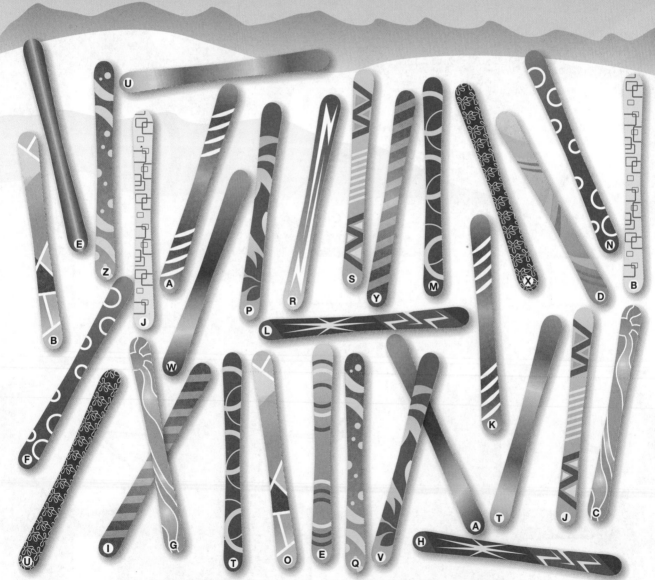

Write the letters from the unmatched skis in the spaces below.

____ ____ ____ ____

_____ **Valley**

Unscramble the letters to learn the name of a popular skiing spot!

UTAH'S STATE SYMBOLS

The beehive became Utah's official state emblem in 1959.
The symbol represents "industry, thrift, and perseverance."

```
        B Z E C U R P S E U L B
      R H D M G Y O K W N V F S L X
    S P O F U O J A A C X R U Q Y O R
    J X N C Q I P R I L E R M N K F C A
    E B R E I K Y U S X D U J T E P W N S F
    T E O Y F K Y R V U A B G Y V R J Y L C
    X E Y B V U A M T S Y F S X O E X A U
  T J H P E R O C U O P N J X Q H T I M P J
  I C I Z E P K T L X U T O U I C R E U Y Z
  P A V S L Y I L W F X N K F U T O V Q B T
  X Y E K R T A N X P A I T Z E U X P C X I
  Z R X S S A R G E C I R N A I D N I P F U
  T R Y F A J X D R Y C P S W I E B G B E P
  X E Z I T L N U O G O V M R Q N U D X Z R
  D H E L Q K M W F X U E X J G Y E P K M S
  C A L I F O R N I A G U L L E A L X Z
  E B I A C E V N P U D Y H N R E G K I
  M X K W M Z R B G Y O L U A A J O G L
    Z I U C D J S X N V K W F T R Y Q
      L R P S Q U A R E D A N C E X
        J Y G Q M A F P U Y Z N O I
          O A B X W G D M J C
            L Q Y M V K S P
```

FIND THESE WORDS

Complete the word search to learn more of Utah's state symbols!

ROCKY MOUNTAIN ELK state animal

CALIFORNIA GULL state bird

DUTCH OVEN state cooking pot

BEEHIVE state emblem

ALLOSAURUS state fossil

CHERRY state fruit

HONEY BEE state insect

COPPER state mineral

SQUARE DANCE state folk dance

INDIAN RICEGRASS state grass

COAL state rock

VERMONT

The Green Mountain State ✳

Capital: **Montpelier** ✳ Abbreviation: **VT**
14th State: **Joined March 4, 1791**

HIKING THROUGH VERMONT!

The Green Mountains run through the middle of Vermont, starting from the border of Massachusetts and continuing up to the border of Canada. You can cross through the mountains following one of the oldest long distance hiking trails in the USA.

COMPLETE THE MAZE!

Along the maze's correct path, you'll pass by some trees marked with letters. Collect the letters from start to finish to complete the sentence below.

START △

FINISH ▷

The _____ _____ _____ _____   _____ _____ _____ _____ _____
is more than 270 miles long. It crosses through many of the highest peaks, marshes, and waterfalls in the Green Mountains.

Let's Draw!

The northern leopard frog is Vermont's official amphibian. Follow the steps to draw one on a blank sheet of paper.

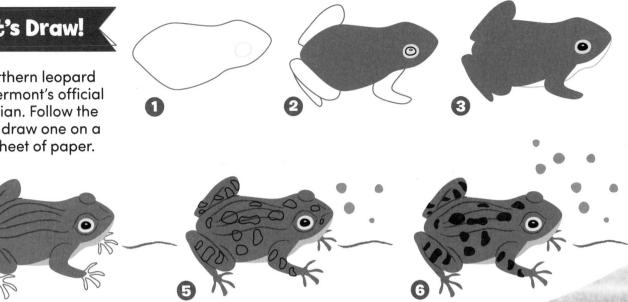

SNOW GOLF!

English writer Rudyard Kipling is believed to have invented the game of snow golf. In 1892, he married an American woman and moved to Vermont. Even though Vermont had long winters, Kipling was determined to continue playing his favorite sport: golf. One day, he painted his golf balls red and ventured into the snow. That's how snow golf was born.

Solve the symbol puzzle to find out what famous book Kipling was writing when he invented snow golf.

Every column must contain each of these symbols:

 Snowshoes   Golf club

 Golf ball    Cup

These symbols must appear only once in each row and column.

When you fill in the charts, match the symbols in the shaded squares (going from left to right) to the correct symbol combination below. The correct combination will reveal the name of the book that Kipling wrote while in Vermont.

 The Man Who Would Be King   *The Jungle Book*   *Just So Stories*

VIRGINIA
✳ The Old Dominion ✳

REED BY REED!

Some of the first structures in present-day America were built by Native Americans in eastern states like Virginia. Saplings were used to build frames, which were then covered by mats of woven reeds.

Women were often the builders, collecting the materials and shaping them into strong structures to protect themselves and their families. The shelters could last many years, with the materials often reused for new projects when the communities grew or moved location.

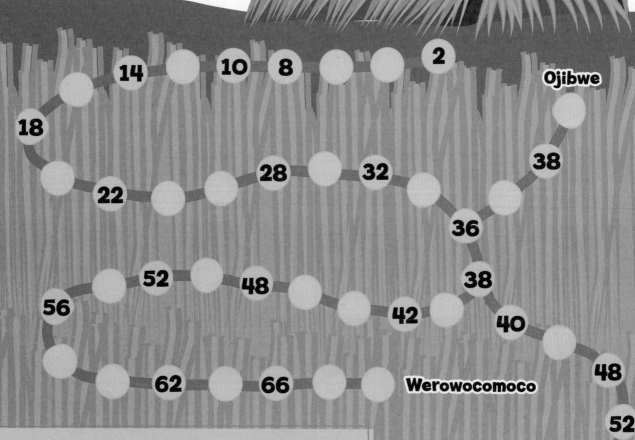

14   10   8   2

Ojibwe

18

22   28   32   38

36

52   48   38

56   42   40

62   66   Werowocomoco   48

52

Complete the pattern of numbers woven through the reeds. Follow the correct path to learn the name of a village where the Algonquian tribe built structures like this before Virginia became a state.

Powhatan 64

92

COASTAL WETLANDS

Virginia's southeastern coast is lined with a chain of islands.
Ocean waves crash around these islands, creating wetlands
and marshes along the state's shoreline.

Use the descriptions below to identify each plant name and its location – in the high marsh
or low marsh. Then mark each plant in the wetlands scene with its corresponding letter.

Saltgrass grows in the high marsh and is a primary source of food for water birds like the gull-billed tern. Saltgrass is known for its tall stalks. **Sea lavender** grows in the low marsh near murky, shallow water. Its lavender flowers have a papery texture. Also found in the low marsh, **eastern grasswort** is known for its simple, curved green leaves.

Saltmeadow hay grows in the high marsh where it's protected from flooding. It can be identified by the clumps of seeds that grow at the tips of its stalks on one side only.

A

Plant Name _____

Location _____

B

Plant Name _____

Location _____

C

Plant Name _____

Location _____

D

Plant Name _____

Location _____

WASHINGTON
✳ The Evergreen State ✳

Capital: **Olympia** ✳ Abbreviation: **WA**
42nd State: **Joined November 11, 1889**

Columbian
Black-tailed Deer

AMAZING WILDLIFE!

The national parks in Washington are home to many unique animals. Some animals, such as the Olympic marmot and Olympic short-tailed weasel, are endemic to Washington, which means they don't live anywhere else in the world.

Olympic Marmot

Olympic Short-tailed
Weasel

WASHINGTON'S NATIONAL PARKS

To learn the names of three national parks in Washington, match the numbers underneath the blanks to the numbers in the secret code.

A	B	C	D	E	F	G	H	I	J	K	L	M	N	O	P	Q	R	S	T	U	V	W	X	Y	Z
20	12	6	17	10	25	16	26	23	24	9	11	1	3	19	2	14	8	4	18	22	13	5	21	7	15

Steller's Jay

1. In Mount ___ ___ ___ ___ ___ ___ ___ National Park, we spotted a
        8 20 23 3 23 10 8

Steller's jay, a Columbian black-tailed deer, and even a black bear.

2. In ___ ___ ___ ___ ___ ___ ___ National Park, we spotted a rhinoceros
     19 11 7 1 2 23 6

auklet, an Olympic short-tailed weasel, and an Olympic marmot.

3. In North ___ ___ ___ ___ ___ ___ ___ ___ National Park, we spotted a
          6 20 4 6 20 17 10 4

pika, a bald eagle, and a mountain goat.

Rhinoceros
Auklet

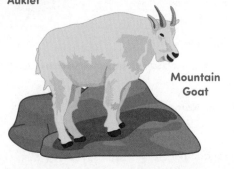

Mountain
Goat

Bald Eagle

Pika

Black Bear

94

DISCOVERING VOLCANOES

There are five major volcanoes in Washington: Mount Baker, Glacier Peak, Mount Rainier, Mount St. Helens, and Mount Adams. All of them are considered active, which means eruptions are possible. Mount Rainier is also the tallest peak in Washington.

Find the volcanic terms in the word search below.

PARTS OF A STRATOVOLCANO

ERUPTION COLUMN

Volcanic bomb

Vent

Debris avalanche

Conduit

Lahar

Magma

WORD SEARCH

```
Z A S X F W R R K B C N Q H T X U D Q G A D Z M S B C D C S
S X K N I X D E B R I S A V A L A N C H E V E D Q M R X H D
D L U P O J Y O P S U W H U E S M T P N U M W N U O W X F I
R N L O N A C L O V D L E I H S L A H A R U H A G B R S R X
E B I V T J K Z K J W L S V U T F K G Y T H H D B C C A V P
N M U L O C N O I T P U R E I X O U K M S V O N F I M F B I
E F U V P D T B B U A Y N U B L G Y X R A E N V S N E K A R
X O V R V H K F A T D R D S M S Z Y V B D N A Y R A M T A S
I L M Q C S C T C C H N J X X F U D V W Z T Q P B C C H W Y
T Y J H C Q H S L A O Y K Z E O N T J O A B K W D L V A P R
S T R A T O V O L C A N O L P V I T D X D J L T L O D P N W
O N A C L O V E N O C R E D N I C V O L U K I A R V Z Y K F
```

STRATOVOLCANO type of volcano composed of layers of hardened lava and ash. It has a conical structure with steep upper slopes. Washington volcanoes are stratovolcanoes.

SHIELD VOLCANO type of volcano composed only of hardened lava. It has gentle slopes and looks like a warrior's shield. There are many shield volcanoes in Hawaii.

CINDER CONE VOLCANO type of volcano shaped like a cone. Made up of hardened lava, a cinder cone volcano is usually no higher than 1,000 feet. They can be found all over the USA.

MAGMA molten (liquid) mixture of rock and gases that causes a volcanic eruption. Magma is found in magma chambers underneath the surface of the Earth.

LAHAR mudflow created during an eruption. It is composed of debris and water.

VENT opening in a volcano through which hot lava escapes to the surface.

CONDUIT channel in the middle of a volcano through which magma flows to the surface.

ERUPTION COLUMN vertical column of ash that erupts from a conduit.

DEBRIS AVALANCHE landslide made up of a large volume of rocks and trees.

VOLCANIC BOMB molten rock that flies out from a volcano during an eruption. Depending on the force of an eruption, some bombs land miles away.

TYPES OF VOLCANOES

Using the volcano descriptions for stratovolcano, shield volcano, and cinder cone volcano, label each photo with the volcano type featured.

A. Wizard Island, Oregon
_____

B. Mauna Kea, Hawaii
_____

C. Mount Rainier, Washington
_____

WEST VIRGINIA
✳ The Mountain State ✳

Capital: **Charleston** ✳ Abbreviation: **WV**
35th State: **Joined June 20, 1863**

HARPERS FERRY NATIONAL HISTORICAL PARK

is a small community located where the Potomac and Shenandoah Rivers meet. The town was the site of a variety of important events during the Civil War, including battles, raids, and meetings. Today, archaeologists studying Harpers Ferry continue to uncover artifacts from Civil War times and beyond.

HIDDEN OBJECTS

Ceramic pot fragment
(used for washing and cooking)

Iron skillet
(used for cooking)

Sledgehammer head
(used for building)

Brick pattern
(floor of the blacksmith's shop)

Lightning rod
(used to prevent fires)

Cast iron fire hydrant
(used to extinguish fires)

Rasp file
(tool from the armory)

Wrench made from broken files
(tool from the armory)

Apothecary scale
(used for measuring medicine)

Broken plate
(made to commemorate the B&O railroad)

WINTER IN THE APPALACHIANS!

During the winter, West Virginia's Appalachian Mountains are covered in snow. The mountainsides and peaks turn white, making West Virginia the perfect place for snow sports. People put on their winter jackets and ride down snowy slopes on skis, snowboards, sleds, and more. Snowtubing is a popular winter sport. It's similar to sledding, except instead of a sled, you slide down the mountain on an inflatable inner tube.

SEARCH WORDS

West Virginia Parks and Resorts

- Snowshoe Mountain
- Elk River
- Pipestem Resort
- Canaan Valley
- Oglebay Resort
- Winterplace
- Timberline Resort
- Blackwater Falls
- White Grass Resort

```
W  I  N  T  E  R  P  L  A  C  E  E  U  N  B  P  B  J
A  H  T  I  M  B  E  R  O  I  N  E  R  N  S  R  O  R  T
M  B  I  P  E  R  F  N  A  L  T  M  A  L  Q  R  L  S  R
A  L  A  C  A  X  E  Y  A  D  P  T  A  F  E  E  Y  P
D  R  A  I  A  G  U  T  C  R  F  W  G  B  M  L  M  O  I
R  E  K  H  N  X  X  C  W  A  H  P  W  V  B  J  J  R  W  P
E  Y  W  T  R  X  C  W  A  F  U  E  R  B  U  A  J  I  H  E
Y  A  A  I  P  A  U  M  S  S  T  N  V  A  R  F  I  S
L  T  W  D  R  P  I  V  L  D  Q  R  E  D  R  M  O  S
T  E  L  K  R  A  Z  M  E  S  E  R  W  F  R  A  T
O  R  Z  W  A  I  T  M  M  R  I  E  S  R  M  R  E
F  F  E  S  D  Z  T  E  S  L  L  S  B  P  N
P  A  H  N  R  L  H  J  G  O  E  U  T  A  T  V
S  L  G  P  O  Y  Z  K  S  R  L  S  M  W  E  I
X  A  L  I  I  O  B  R  E  N  K  O  E  R  R  T  N
A  L  T  R  F  A  R  D  R  Q  T  M  V  E  O
T  S  O  T  G  D  P  N  C  T  D  D  E  X  A  U
D  L  L  R  E  B  A  Y  R  E  S  O  R  T  Y  N
O  G  L  E  B  A  Y  R  E  S  O  R  T
```

After completing the word search, fill in the blanks below with the letters marked by colored inner tubes within your circled answers. Write them in the order in which they appear in the word search from left to right and top to bottom.

One of the best places to snowtube is Snowshoe Mountain, which is located in the

____ ____ ____ ____ ____ ____ ____ ____ ____

Mountains (a portion of the Appalachians).

WISCONSIN
✳ The Badger State ✳

Capital: **Madison** ✳ Abbreviation: **WI**
30th State: **Joined May 29, 1848**

SKIING THE BIRKIE

Held in Cable, Wisconsin, the American Birkebeiner is a famous cross-country skiing event that consists of a series of races nicknamed the Birkie. (Cross-country skiing is a type of skiing done on flat surfaces.)

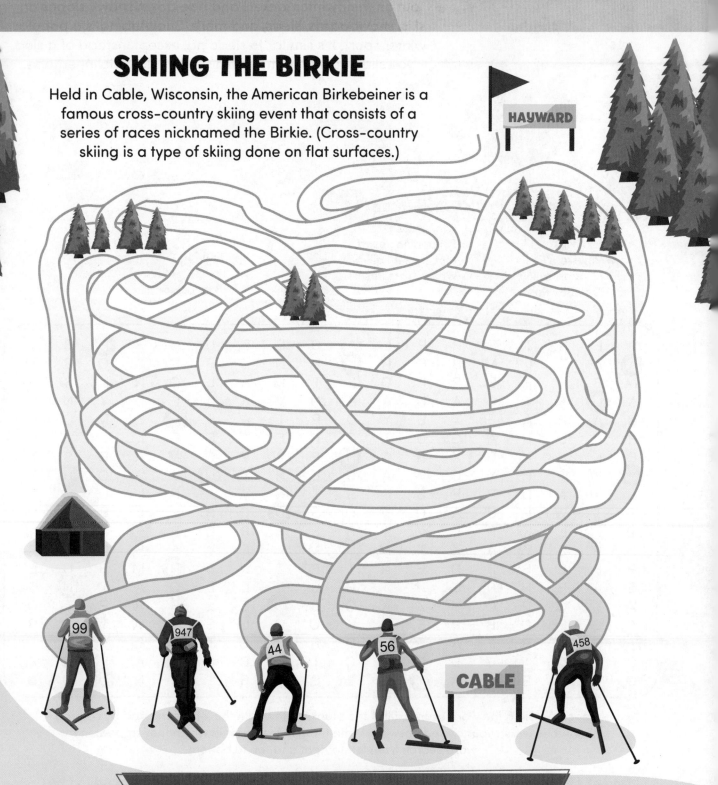

From Cable to Hayward, the longest race spans a distance of 34 miles. These five skiers were the best!
Complete the maze to see which skier made it to Hayward first.

THE AMERICAN BADGER

THE AMERICAN BADGER is Wisconsin's state animal. Some people think the badger got its name from the unique white stripe on its head, which looks like a badge. Others think the name "badge" comes from the French word that means "to dig." The badger catches most of its food by digging underground.

A   B   C   D   E

Which Badger Is Different?

Circle the badger that is different from the other four. The different badger's letter will complete the sentence below.

Wisconsin's nickname is the Badger State because...

A. there are many badgers in Wisconsin.

B. the sight of miners digging tunnels into hillsides reminded people of badgers.

C. badgers look pretty.

D. badgers are fighters.

E. badgers have long noses.

AMERICA'S DAIRYLAND

Wisconsin makes hundreds of different cheeses. Local farmers believe Wisconsin cheese is special because cows in the area graze on high-quality grass.

WORD SEARCH

Circle some favorite cheeses from Wisconsin.

GORGONZOLA
BRIE
BABY SWISS
MOZZARELLA
CHEDDAR

```
            A Z R E M T
          C O F W X L B Y G N S U H
    B I N J R D Y C L N P K O S G V B
    A J B I M V X E B O C I D K V S P
    B D L O P Q R F R N J H Z D E P F L
    Y T Z X K A B M I Y S Z E N O B M T
    S P O L Z N J A E V Q K A D F I J D
    W Y S Z F I X T D L O U X P D U A P
    I G O R G O N Z O L A B I V N A S
    S M K V D T M I F D J A P L Y T R
    S A M J I P O L N D Q V O I K M F
```

Capital: Cheyenne ✵ **Abbreviation: WY**
44th State: Joined July 10, 1890

In Cheyenne,
CARRIAGES AND WAGONS
are displayed in museums to teach visitors about transportation of the past.

1. This carriage got its name from the carriages used for hunting with canines in England. In Cheyenne, pioneers used the carriage to get around town.

A **F O U R** __ __ __ __ __ __ __ __ __ __ __ CART
  M T O Z A L J J E J G G T N

2. This wagon was used on dairy farms, such as the Plains Dairy in Cheyenne. It delivered milk from the farms to homes and shops.

A __ __ __ __ __ __ __ __ __
  P S E V A R N T F

3. This wagon was used to carry food and cooking supplies. It was also used to deliver food to cowboys working on Wyoming's ranches.

A __ __ __ __ __ __ __ __ __ __
  U L O U V A R N T F

4. This carriage was used to transport up to nine passengers at a time across the Overland Trail.

THE __ __ __ __ __ __ __
    T H J Z E R F G
__ __ __ __ __ __ __ __
Q X R N J U T R U L

5. This wagon was popular with festival goers. Used during festivals and parades, the wagon has a rotating drum for "popping" a delicious snack.

A __ __ __ __ __ __ __ __ __ __
  Y T Y U T Z F A R N T F

Alphabet Key

W	Y	Z	J	L	N	D	V	B	E	X	H	F	G	U	M	S	A	I	O	C	K	Q	T	P	R
A	B	C	D	E	F	G	H	I	J	K	L	M	N	O	P	Q	R	S	T	U	V	W	X	Y	Z

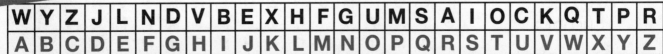

PRONGHORNS

Wyoming has the largest population of pronghorns in the USA. Pronghorns are some of the fastest land animals in North America. They can run close to 60 miles per hour.

Traveling about 300 miles annually from northern Wyoming to Grand Teton and back, pronghorns make one of the longest land migrations of any land animals in North America.

SPOT THE DIFFERENCE!

Pronghorns are beautiful hoofed animals. They are named after their horns. Each horn splits to form small forward-pointing prongs. Find and circle the 10 differences between the two animals we saw.

Starting from left to right, collect the letters hidden in the grass to complete the following sentence.

A hoofed animal is called an

____ ____ _____ ___ ___.

WASHINGTON, D.C.
✳ The Nation's Capital ✳

U.S. Capital
Founded July 16, 1790

MARYLAND

WASHINGTON, D.C.

WEST VIRGINIA

VIRGINIA

MARYLAND OR VIRGINIA?

Washington, D.C., the national capital of the USA, is home of the White House, where the president lives. D.C. isn't actually part of any other state. Located between Maryland and Virginia, the city is formally called the District of Columbia and is governed by the US Congress instead of a state government.

THE WASHINGTON MONUMENT is located at the
National Mall, which is home to many historical monuments. The white tower (called an obelisk) honors President George Washington, who was born in Virginia.

Let's Draw!

Follow the steps on the right and draw the Washington Monument!

George Washington was the first president of the United States.

❶ ❷ ❸ ❹

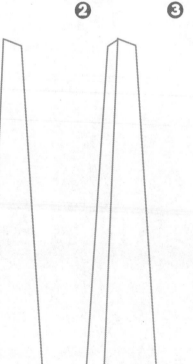
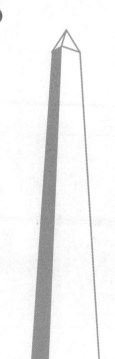
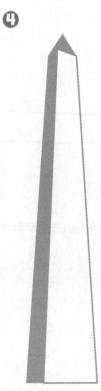

Washington Monument

THE JEFFERSON MEMORIAL

stands at the southern end of the National Mall and features a bronze statue of Thomas Jefferson. The building is designed after the Pantheon in Rome. Famous quotes and excerpts from the Declaration of Independence are etched into the marble walls.

Thomas Jefferson was the third president of the United States.

Let's Draw!

Grab a pencil and draw the Jefferson Memorial below!

①

②

③

④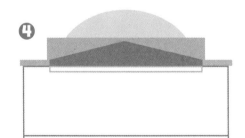

⑤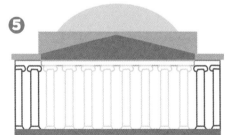

⑥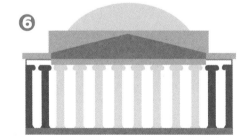

⑦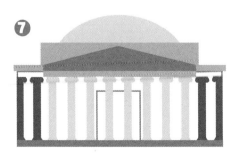

⑧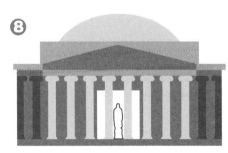

⑨

The Jefferson Memorial

ANSWER KEY

ALABAMA PAGES 2-3

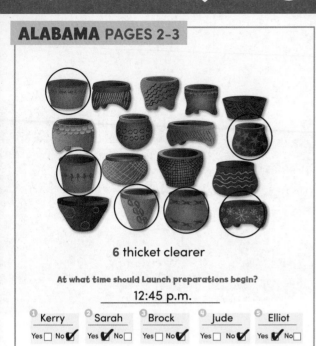

6 thicket clearer

At what time should Launch preparations begin?

__12:45 p.m.__

① Kerry Yes ☐ No ☑
② Sarah Yes ☑ No ☐
③ Brock Yes ☐ No ☑
④ Jude Yes ☐ No ☑
⑤ Elliot Yes ☑ No ☐

ALASKA PAGES 4-5

What causes the aurora borealis?

15 stars = ice crystals sparkling within clouds

25 stars = moonlight reflecting off the ice of glaciers and icebergs

35 stars = particles from the sun reacting with gases in the atmosphere

45 stars = solar activity far off in space

ARIZONA PAGES 6-7

19 14 7 21

61 – The Painted Desert

ARKANSAS PAGES 8-9

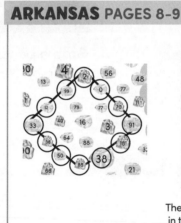

$(12 \times 10) - 35 = 85$
$(9 \div 9) \times 50 = 50$
$(8 - 5) \times 12 = 36$
$(5 + 28) \times 1 = 33$
$(0 \times 83) + 12 = 12$
$(56 - 23) \times 3 = 99$
$11 + 73 - 82 = 2$
$(45 \div 3) - 15 = 0$
$(86 + 7) - 23 = 70$
$(9 \times 3) + 64 = 91$
$(33 \div 11) + 15 = 18$
$92 - 15 - 39 = 38$

The largest diamond found in the Crater of Diamonds weighed 16.37 carats.

Jeff   Lucy   Tim   Mia   Mitch

CALIFORNIA PAGES 10-11

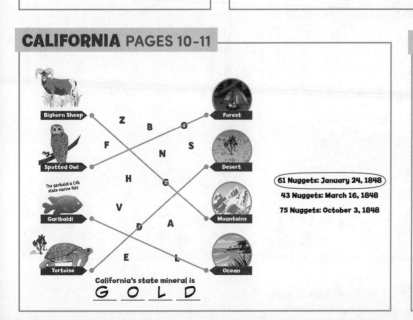

Bighorn Sheep
Spotted Owl
The garibaldi is CA's state marine fish!
Garibaldi
Tortoise

Forest
Desert
Mountains
Ocean

Z B G
F N S
H G
V A
D
E L

61 Nuggets: January 24, 1848
43 Nuggets: March 16, 1848
75 Nuggets: October 3, 1848

California's state mineral is

__G O L D__

COLORADO PAGES 12-13

Hummingbirds Mesa Verde National Park
Bighorn sheep Rocky Mountain National Park
Tiger salamanders Black Canyon of the Gunnison National Park
Kangaroo rats Great Sand Dunes National Park

Crossword:
⁶C R I B³
      A
¹S A N D A L S
H   K
A   ⁷F I R E T
⁴M A T
P
²S O A P
O

CONNECTICUT PAGES 14-15

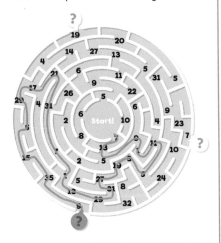

Trees in Group 1 are called deciduous trees.
Trees in Group 2 are called evergreen trees.

DELAWARE PAGES 16-17

1	6	5	7	9	4	2	3	8
4	8	7	3	1	2	9	5	6
9	3	2	8	5	6	7	1	4
8	1	3	4	7	5	6	9	2
5	7	6	2	3	9	4	8	1
2	4	9	6	8	1	3	7	5
3	2	1	5	6	7	8	4	9
6	9	8	1	4	3	5	2	7
7	5	4	9	2	8	1	6	3

Fun fact #4 is not true.

B
C
A
C
C

The University of Delaware's
Blue Hens

FLORIDA PAGES 18-19

How many bird species live in the Everglades?
18 birds spotted = More than **300** species!

Where NASA sends rockets and astronauts	S P A C E
Something that isn't being used; extra	S P A R E
To look at something or someone intensely	S T A R E
Not new or fresh; an old piece of bread	S T A L E
A strong post or spike used to anchor a tent	S T A K E
A slithery reptile that doesn't have limbs	S N A K E
Something to nibble on between meals	S N A C K
When a rope is loose; the opposite of taut	S L A C K
Smooth or slippery, and usually wet	S L I C K
A single piece of bread	S L I C E
Something to add flavor to food	S P I C E
Where NASA sends rockets and astronauts	S P A C E

GEORGIA PAGES 20-21

T A A L A T N — H S N V A A N A
A T L A N T A — S A V A N N A H

The capital of Georgia is . . .

This city is known for its old oak trees that are often draped with Spanish moss.

S I S I S P M I S I P
M I S S I S S I P P I

R E V I R
R I V E R

Georgia is one of the largest states east of the . . .

T R I N M A — U E H T R L
M A R T I N — L U T H E R

I N G K — R J
K I N G — J R

This civil rights leader was born in Georgia, and his legacy lives on today through everyone fighting for racial equality.

Peanuts aren't the only nuts grown in the Peach State!

More **P E C A N S** are harvested in Georgia than in any other state, mostly in the months of October and November.

HAWAII PAGES 22-23

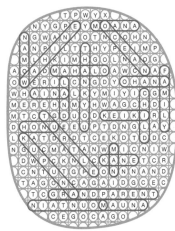

IDAHO PAGES 24-25

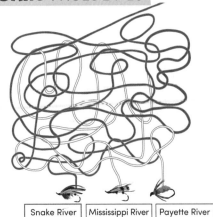

1. Rocky Mountains
2. Bogus Basin
3. Boise River
4. World Center for Birds of Prey
5. Anne Frank Human Rights Memorial
6. Idaho Botanical Garden
7. Boise National Forest
8. Julia Davis Park
9. Lucky Peak Dam

Snake River | Mississippi River | Payette River

ILLINOIS PAGES 26-27

$\bullet + \text{🍕} = \boxed{5}$

$\text{🌸} - \text{◎} = \boxed{4}$ $\boxed{5} + \boxed{4} + \boxed{6} = $
$\underline{\qquad 15 \qquad}$

$\bigcirc \times \bullet = \boxed{6}$

1	3	6	2	4	7	5	8	9
2	5	8	3	1	9	4	7	6
4	7	9	5	6	8	3	2	1
6	9	4	1	7	3	2	5	8
8	1	5	4	9	2	6	3	7
3	2	7	6	8	5	9	1	4
5	4	1	8	2	6	7	9	3
7	6	2	9	3	1	8	4	5
9	8	3	7	5	4	1	6	2

Facts 1, 3, and 5 are true.

INDIANA PAGES 28-29

The dunes are made of "_____" sand, which makes a unique sound when walked on. — **GLACIERS**

The dunes were created by receding _____. — **SINGING**

The dunes are located near Lake _____. — **CROSSROADS**

Indiana's state motto is "the "_____ of America." — **MICHIGAN**

Indianapolis hosts a famous auto race called the ____ 500. — **INDY**

IOWA PAGES 30-31

3 differences: The Netherlands grows more tulips than any other country in the world. The tulip is one of the symbols of Dutch culture.

KANSAS PAGES 32-33

The Knork Mike Miller
The Flying Machine William J. Purvis
Basketball James Naismith
The ICEE Machine Omar Knedlik

1. B L A C K B I R D .
2. A P O L L O
3. M E T E O R I T E ,
4. R O C K E T S .
5. S A L L Y   R I D E .

KENTUCKY PAGES 34-35

	Answers	Jockeys		
		Jim	Carol	Paul
Horses	Fancy Feet	X	✓	X
	Happy-Go-Lucky	✓	X	X
	Fearless	X	X	✓
Results	1st Place	X	X	✓
	2nd Place	✓	X	X
	3rd Place	X	✓	X

The fireworks show that kicks off the Kentucky Derby is called <u>THUNDER</u> Over Louisville.

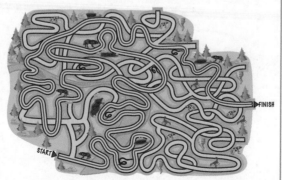

Types of Obstacles: <u>3</u> (wolf, snake, thick mud)
<u>Odd</u> fact is true.

LOUISIANA PAGES 36-37

Red-headed Woodpecker

Brown Pelican

Vermilion Flycatcher

American Coot

Wood Duck

MAINE PAGES 38–39

MARYLAND PAGES 40–41

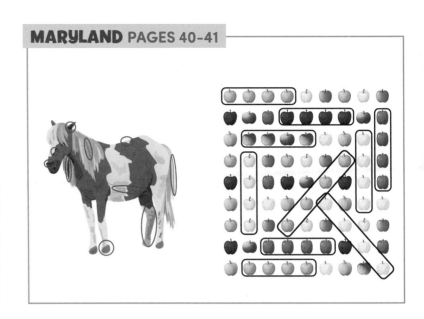

MASSACHUSETTS PAGES 42–43

Sannup   M A N

Squaw   W O M A N

Cone   S U N

Mishoon   B O A T

Wetu   H O U S E

Wobsacuck   E A G L E

Ausupp   R A C C O O N

Nitchicke   H A N D

```
R A I T M O Y   R N
R A U S U P P B O I
A R E F S B S U N T
C E X I P H Q X U C
C T U N I T R D N H
O U N C B W E A B I
O K O R A F Z W L C
N U Q O A Z W B A K
G A U A T N F B A Z E
O S S A H U N O B S A O
G A N Z G R J P Z S C C
T L N E U N E L A K U Q
A R S A C L Y E X U N
W M S S W S V C C N
M A S N E K K H R B
R L F C Q T V H
S R N O D A O O
C A C R S E H N
P L   H O U S E I
Y
```

MICHIGAN PAGES 44–45

```
                    ¹F
              ²B L O S S O M
        ³D E E R       X
              R
              I
       ⁴T U R T L E
        I     G
        G    ⁵R
       ⁶S T O N E
        R     B
       ⁷W I N D M I L ⁸L
                    A
                    K
                    E
```

MINNESOTA PAGES 46–47

```
7 28634  96 1208 423  964  82 10 2685 4  7 620 432
SWILFD TRCICE ISA QAN AQBUATIUC OGRASVS

1 496528  2 306 8 4  07 214 44 890  6 12 84 72 38 4
NTCHIAT GBROWS BGEDST IDN SFHALELZOW

7 2 56 4290  5 07 26 23  6180 54 12 6 26 95 4 3 40
YWGATEAR. BWEHEND TFHE XPHROPHKHEWCY

4 9262 108  4 76 212 70 4  852 4 6 1089 2  6 34
SNPEARKS OWF FJOZOD GIROWVINAG OXN

6 78204  7 8 1628  9 4 10 25462 6 812 904  5 21 4830 28
WTATER, KMXANY MBCELKIEVE TLHCIS NRNEFJERS

6 3 4  9 628 50  7 041 62  4 9 62 452  0 182 3 0 2964
TAO RWILSD QRISCE, WGHICTH HUAS VBENEN

4 2 20586265  3 8  1 492  6 124 36726  27 4  128 20 67 4 98
HARVLESTEDWD XBZY NUATBIAVE AHMCERICAFRNGS

562 1 228 9 2601 272 4  105 8 2  32 7 62 90 2 264 1 25
AIN RMINONESKOETA AFQOR LCMENRTURIEMSR.
```

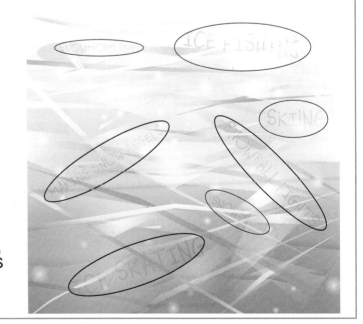

MISSISSIPPI PAGES 48-49

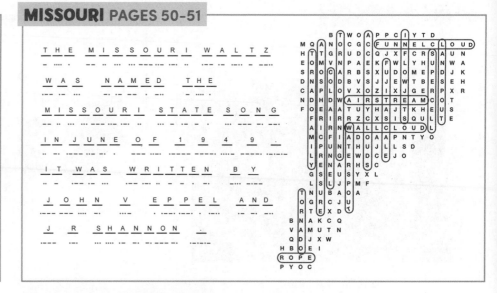

MISSOURI PAGES 50-51

THE MISSOURI WALTZ

WAS NAMED THE

MISSOURI STATE SONG

IN JUNE OF 1949.

IT WAS WRITTEN BY

JOHN V EPPEL AND

J R SHANNON .

MONTANA PAGES 52-53

35 - "Gold and Silver"

Seismosaurus

Tyrannosaurus rex

Maiasaura

Triceratops

Gryposaurus

Plesiosaur   Hadrosaur

The study of dinosaurs is called Paleontology

NEBRASKA PAGES 54-55

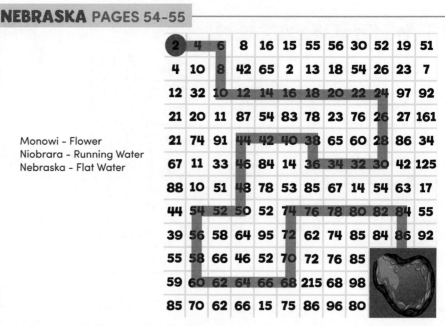

Monowi - Flower
Niobrara - Running Water
Nebraska - Flat Water

NEVADA PAGES 56-57

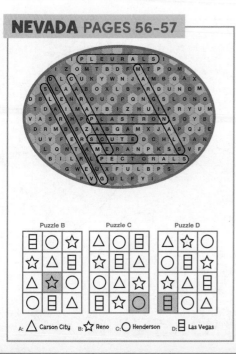

Puzzle B   Puzzle C   Puzzle D

A: △ Carson City   B: ☆ Reno   C: ◯ Henderson   D: ▤ Las Vegas

NEW HAMPSHIRE PAGES 58-59

Birch leaves: $\frac{3}{5}$
Ash leaves: $\frac{2}{5}$
Oak leaves: $\frac{3}{4}$
Beech leaves: $\frac{4}{10}$

NAOINUSTM → MOUNTAINS

HEASCEB RTSSEOF → BEACHES FORESTS

DMAFNALR SELKA → FARMLAND LAKES

SMASRTE OSPLSE → STREAMS SLOPES

ICETPMSAS → CAMPSITES

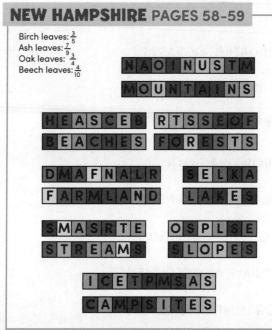

snowflake + wood plank = snowboard
snowflake + ski + = snowmobile
snowflake + shoe = snowshoe
snowflake + ball = snowball
snowflake + cone = snow cone
snowflake + angel = snow angel
snowflake + shovel = snow shovel

108

NEW JERSEY PAGES 60-61

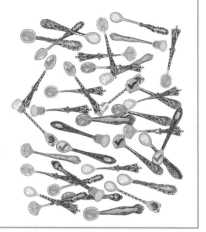

NEW MEXICO PAGES 62-63

NEW YORK PAGES 64-65

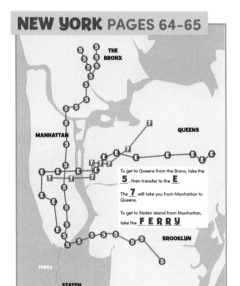

To get to Queens from the Bronx, take the **5**, then transfer to the **E**.

The **7** will take you from Manhattan to Queens.

To get to Staten Island from Manhattan, take the **FERRY**.

NORTH CAROLINA PAGES 66-67

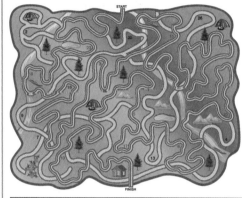

1. T H E   B L O W I N G   R O C K
   18 26 12   20 8 19 3 10 6 11   5 19 17 9

2. C R A G G Y   G A R D E N S
   17 5 23 11 11 7   11 20 5 18 12 6 4

3. G R A N D F A T H E R Mountain
   11 5 23 6 16 25 23 18 26 12 5

4. T H E   B R I N E G A R Cabin
   18 26 12   20 5 10 6 12 11 23 5

5. L O O K I N G   G L A S S Rock
   8 19 19 9 10 6 11   11 8 23 4 4

23	20	17	16	12	25	11	26	10	24	9	8	1	6	19	2	14	5	4	18	22	13	3	21	7	15
A	B	C	D	E	F	G	H	I	J	K	L	M	N	O	P	Q	R	S	T	U	V	W	X	Y	Z

NORTH DAKOTA PAGES 68

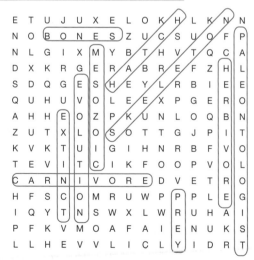

7:00 11:45 1:15 3:35 1:30 12:45
L A K O T A

9:25 11:45 1:15 3:35   7:55 4:05 5:20 11:45
M A K O   S I C A

7:00 11:45 1:15 3:35 1:30 11:45
L A K O T A

OHIO PAGES 70-71

The <u>Queen</u> <u>City</u>

B   C   A   D

OKLAHOMA PAGES 72-73

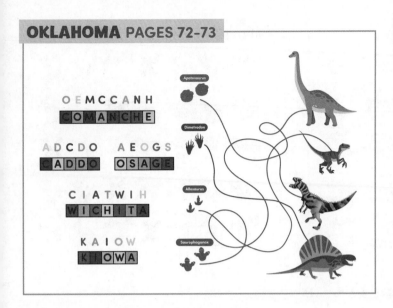

O E M C C A N H
COMANCHE

A D C D O   A E O G S
CADDO   **OSAGE**

C I A T W I H
WICHITA

K A I O W
KIOWA

OREGON PAGES 74-75

The most famous sea stack is called <u>Haystack Rock.</u>

PENNSYLVANIA PAGES 76-77

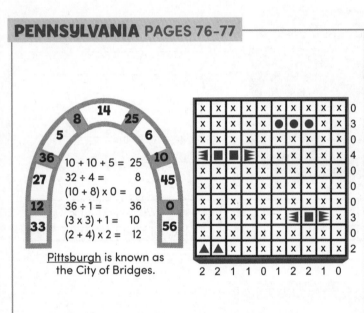

10 + 10 + 5 = 25
32 ÷ 4 = 8
(10 + 8) x 0 = 0
36 ÷ 1 = 36
(3 x 3) + 1 = 10
(2 + 4) x 2 = 12

<u>Pittsburgh</u> is known as the City of Bridges.

RHODE ISLAND PAGES 78-79

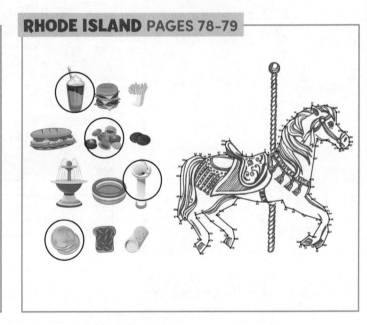

SOUTH CAROLINA PAGES 80-81

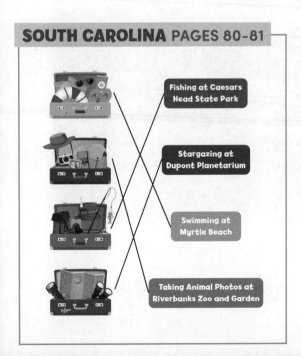

Fishing at Caesars Head State Park

Stargazing at Dupont Planetarium

Swimming at Myrtle Beach

Taking Animal Photos at Riverbanks Zoo and Garden

SOUTH DAKOTA PAGES 82-83

4   2   1   3

The South Dakota state bird is the **RING-NECKED PHEASANT**

TENNESSEE PAGES 84-85

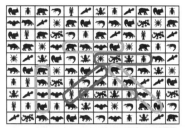

1 group: Cave dwellers are called "troglobites."
2 groups: Cave lovers are called "troglophiles."
3 groups: Cave guests are called "trogloxenes."

		8	105	25	30	35	40	52	11	55
		32	56	20	114	14	45	100	26	5
		5	10	15	110	177	50	234	15	96
15	20	19	54	216	48	74	195	55	36	200	146
105	95	90	85	80	75	70	65	60	64	86	34
85	100	43	59	184	14	61	105	55	74	24	125
59	105	118	300	73	100	37	67	0	213	63	19
66	110	115	120	125	130	140	14	54	110	111	87
97	94	150	87	95	135	62	45	112	125	45	33
165	160	155	150	145	140	99	76	85			
170	211	205	21	185	217	215	10	98			
175	180	185	190	195	200	205	210	215			

TEXAS PAGES 86-87

Should I eat Tex-Mex or Texas barbeque? — Question

The first rodeo in the world took place in Pecos, Texas in 1883. — Statement

Did you know Texas was the 28th state to join the union? — Statement

Yeehaw! — Exclamation

Remember the Alamo! — Exclamation

Howdy, partner! — Exclamation

The Texas flag shares its colors with the American flag. — Statement

Look at that armadillo! — Exclamation

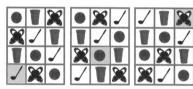

UTAH PAGES 88-89

DEER Valley

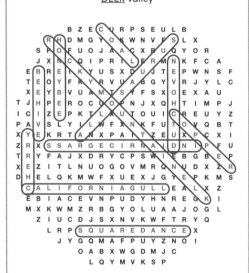

VERMONT PAGES 90-91

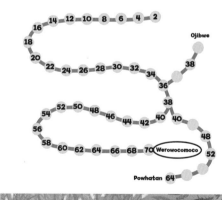

The Long Trail

The Jungle Book

VIRGINIA PAGES 92-93

14 12 10 8 6 4 2
16
18
20
22 24 26 28 30 32 34
Ojibwe
38
36
38
52 50 48
54   46 44 42 40 40
56
58 60 62 64 66 68 70 Werowocomoco
48
52
Powhatan 64

A — Saltgrass / Plant Name / High marsh / Location
D — Sea lavender / Plant Name / Low marsh / Location
C — Eastern grasswort / Plant Name / Low marsh / Location
D — Saltmeadow hay / Plant Name / High marsh / Location

WASHINGTON PAGES 94–95

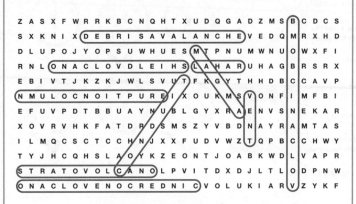

1. Mount <u>Rainier</u> National Park
2. <u>Olympic</u> National Park
3. North <u>Cascades</u> National Park

WEST VIRGINIA PAGES 96–97

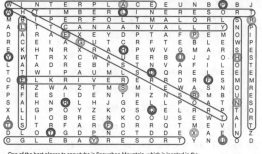

One of the best places to snowtube is Snowshoe Mountain, which is located in the
<u>A L L E G H E N Y</u> Mountains (a portion of the Appalachians).

WISCONSIN PAGES 98–99

B.

Wisconsin's nickname is the Badger State because <u>the sight of miners digging tunnels into hillsides reminded people of badgers.</u>

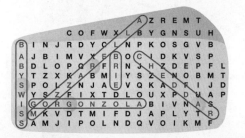

WYOMING PAGES 100–101

1. A FOUR WHEELED DOG CART
2. A MILK WAGON
3. A CHUCKWAGON
4. THE OVERLAND STAGECOACH
5. A POPCORN WAGON

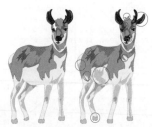

A hoofed animal is called an <u>ungulate</u>.